P9-BYE-201

WITHDRAWN

Should Juveniles
Be Tried as Adults?

Other Books in the At Issue Series:

OPPOSING VIEWPOINTS® SERIES

Should Juveniles Be Tried as Adults?

Christine Watkins, Book Editor

Des Plaines Public Library
1501 Ellinwood Street
Des Plaines, IL. 60016

GREENHAVEN PRESS
A part of Gale, Cengage Learning

GALE
CENGAGE Learning

Detroit • New York • San Francisco • New Haven, Conn • Waterville, Maine • London

Christine Nasso, *Publisher*
Elizabeth Des Chenes, *Managing Editor*

© 2008 Greenhaven Press, a part of Gale, Cengage Learning.

Gale and Greenhaven Press are registered trademarks used herein under license.

For more information, contact:
Greenhaven Press
27500 Drake Rd.
Farmington Hills, MI 48331-3535
Or you can visit our Internet site at gale.cengage.com

ALL RIGHTS RESERVED.
No part of this work covered by the copyright herein may be reproduced, transmitted, stored, or used in any form or by any means graphic, electronic, or mechanical, including but not limited to photocopying, recording, scanning, digitizing, taping, Web distribution, information networks, or information storage and retrieval systems, except as permitted under Section 107 or 108 of the 1976 United States Copyright Act, without the prior written permission of the publisher.

For product information and technology assistance, contact us at

Gale Customer Support, 1-800-877-4253
For permission to use material from this text or product, submit all requests online at www.cengage.com/permissions

Further permissions questions can be emailed to permissionrequest@cengage.com

Articles in Greenhaven Press anthologies are often edited for length to meet page requirements. In addition, original titles of these works are changed to clearly present the main thesis and to explicitly indicate the author's opinion. Every effort is made to ensure that Greenhaven Press accurately reflects the original intent of the authors. Every effort has been made to trace the owners of copyrighted material.

Cover photograph reproduced by permission of Images.com/Corbis.

LIBRARY OF CONGRESS CATALOGING-IN-PUBLICATION DATA

Should juveniles be tried as adults? / Christi Watkins, book editor.
p. cm. -- (At issue)
Includes bibliographical references and index.
ISBN-13: 978-0-7377-4077-6 (hardcover)
ISBN-13: 978-0-7377-4078-3 (pbk.)
1. Juvenile delinquents--United States. 2. Prosecution--United States. 3. Sentences (Criminal procedure)--United States. 4. Community service (Punishment)--United States. 5. Criminal liability--United States. I. Watkins, Christine, 1951-
KF9812.S55 2008
345.73'03--dc22

2008001001

Printed in the United States of America
1 2 3 4 5 6 7 8 12 11 10 09 08

Contents

Introduction

"Old enough to do the crime, old enough to do the time." It is a catchy phrase, but it also represents a departure from the original premise under which the juvenile justice system was created over one hundred years ago—to protect and rehabilitate young criminals. However, because of an epidemic of youth crime that began in the late 1970s, the public demanded a "get tough" approach; as a result, state and federal legislatures lowered the minimum age and expanded the offenses for which youths could be prosecuted in adult courts. The goal was that the fear of harsh punishment would deter juveniles from committing crimes. Recent studies—including many funded by the U.S. Justice Department—have shown, however, that punishment and incarceration may not have been effective in deterring juvenile crime, and may have in fact created more harm than good. According to a 2007 report by the Campaign for Youth Justice, the number of minors held in adult correctional facilities has surged 208 percent since the 1990s, and "youth who are incarcerated in adult facilities are more likely to suffer abuse, become mentally and emotionally ill, and may be rearrested and commit more serious offenses than youth who benefit from the treatment, counseling, and services available through the juvenile justice system." Thus the dilemma: Should the primary goal of juvenile justice be to protect the community from juvenile criminals, or should it be to help juvenile criminals become law-abiding individuals who will contribute to society? Many experts in the field of juvenile justice believe that one does not necessarily have to exclude the other, that there is an approach that can incorporate both of these goals. It is called Balanced and Restorative Justice.

The guiding principle of Balanced and Restorative Justice is for victims, communities, and juvenile offenders to receive balanced attention so that all will benefit from their interactions with the juvenile justice system. The objectives are three-fold: accountability, community safety, and competency development, in which offenders demonstrate marked improvement in their behavior and skills to become productive, responsible citizens. How will these three objectives be obtained? Through the use of community service, say proponents.

Accountability is the essence of Balanced and Restorative Justice. In this system, youth offenders must acknowledge to the victims and community the harm they have caused and must personally commit time and energy to make restitution. Additionally, crime victims are afforded an opportunity to give an impact statement in which they can describe the emotional, physical, and financial effects of the crime and to state what they need in order to feel that the harm they experienced is being repaired. Victims are included (on a strictly voluntary basis) in dialogue sessions with the offenders, juvenile justice officials, and community leaders regarding ways to best provide restitution, such as building a shelter for battered women and rape victims or tearing down crack houses. Participation in the planning, implementation, and evaluation of these community service programs gives the victim a voice and a sense of empowerment, which often helps reduce any short- or long-term trauma, say proponents of such programs.

Community service also addresses the second objective of Balanced and Restorative Justice—safety of the community—by enabling youth, adults, law enforcement, and civic leaders to build meaningful relationships with one another, supporters argue. In his article "Restorative Community Service: Earning Redemption, Gaining Skills, and Proving Worth," writer and community justice expert Dennis Maloney explains,

> "Restorative community service strengthens what criminologists refer to as the 'bond' between youthful offenders and

the community. As offenders take on meaningful roles providing service to others—and as they are treated as a resource rather than a problem—they increase their sense of belonging, usefulness, and attachment to the community. In turn, as the community sees offenders making meaningful contributions, it becomes more accepting and supportive."

Finally, community service proponents believe these programs offer tremendous potential to fulfill the third objective of Balanced and Restorative Justice—competency development. Instead of passively sitting in detention centers being lectured against committing further drug, alcohol, or other legal violations, young criminals are able to get out into the community, accomplish work assignments, and see firsthand the positive impact of their efforts, say Balanced and Restorative Justice supporters. Young lawbreakers learn not only the fundamental skills of following instructions and cooperating with coworkers, argue proponents, they also learn more specific skills like those necessary for landscaping or construction projects. Upon satisfactory completion of their community service commitment, these juvenile offenders can be rewarded with employment referrals or even permanent employment, say those who support such programs.

So, while "old enough to do the crime, old enough to do the time" may be true and appropriate in certain cases, many judges, probation officers, corrections officials, and juvenile justice experts believe Balanced and Restorative Justice may be more effective in the long run for curbing delinquency. As sixteen-year-old Roneka Jenkins, who attends Thurgood Marshall Academy, said, "Young people need opportunities to turn their lives around. . . . We need to give youth the education and skills to get good jobs and contribute to society. That's best for everyone."

Trying juveniles as adults is a hotly debated and challenging issue. The authors in *At Issue: Should Juveniles Be Tried as*

Adults? discuss the legal, ethical, developmental, and emotional factors that surround this important social dilemma.

1

Juveniles Should Not Be Tried in Adult Courts

Hannah McCrea

Hannah McCrea is currently pursuing a master's degree in Environmental Regulation at the London School of Economics. She is a writer for The Seminal, *an independent, collaborative blog that carries political, social, and creative news and viewpoints from university students and young professionals.*

The skyrocketing trend in the United States to get tough on juvenile crime has resulted in an increasing number of minors being tried as adults. In fact, over two hundred thousand minors are charged in adult courts every year. However, juveniles by definition are not adults and therefore should not be treated as such—ever. After all, America's legal system recognizes that the mental competence of children under the age of eighteen has not fully developed, thus minors are not allowed to vote, drink alcohol, or sign legal contracts. In keeping with that concept, juveniles should not be subjected to the physical, emotional, and mental abuse found in adult jails. Instead, they should be sent to juvenile detention centers where they would have a chance at education and rehabilitation.

In May 2000, 13 year-old Nathaniel Brazill, an African-American boy from a low-income Florida family, shot and killed his middle school teacher, Barry Grunow, on the last day of school. A few weeks earlier, also in Florida, 12 year-old Lionel Tate killed his 6 year-old playmate while practicing a wrestling move he saw on television.

Hannah McCrea, "A Double Standard for American Juveniles," *theseminal.com*, June 22, 2007. Copyright © 2007. Reproduced by permission. www.theseminal.com/2007/06/22/a-double-standard-for-american-juveniles.

Both these cases stirred controversy in Florida not because of the senselessness of the crimes, but because of the severity of the punishments: Brazill was convicted of second-degree murder and sentenced to 28 years in prison without the possibility of parole. And Tate was convicted of first-degree murder and sentenced to life in prison without the possibility of parole, making him the youngest person in modern US history to be sentenced to life in prison. Both were tried as adults, and at the ages of 14 and 13 respectively, were locked away in adult prisons to serve their sentences.

Juveniles Are Increasingly Tried as Adults

At the time of their convictions, Florida led the nation in trying minors as adults, a trend that has skyrocketed across America in the past 15 years. Currently [2007], over 200,000 minors are charged in adult courts each year, and in 2005 nearly 7000 minors were being housed in adult jails. More disturbing, a recent series by PBS *Frontline, When Kids Get Life,* reveals that the US is one of only a few countries in the world that sentences minors under the age of 18 to life in prison, and there are 2200 such convicts currently serving life sentences in the US. (According to the advocacy organization Pendulum Foundation, there are only 12 in the rest of the world.) Not until March 2005 did the US Supreme Court finally overturn a previous ruling and outlaw execution for crimes committed by anyone under the age of 18, acknowledging that giving teenagers the death penalty represents "cruel and unusual punishment."

So if the Supreme Court has already ruled that when it comes to execution, minors can't be held accountable to the same extent as adults, why hasn't the entire practice of trying minors as adults come to an end? Why, when minors are minors by definition, should they *ever* be tried as adults?

The sharp increase in minors tried in adult courts is due to a wave of state legislation in the 1990s that gave judges and prosecutors the ability to determine who should be tried as an adult, along with new laws assigning mandatory minimum sentences for certain types of convictions including first- and second-degree murder. In addition, many of the officials making these decisions hold elected positions, which compelled them (and compels them still) to take tough stances against young criminals following America's spike in violent street crime in the early nineties. (This was the case with state attorney Barry Krischer of Florida's affluent Palm Beach County, where Nathaniel Brazill was prosecuted, who defends in this interview his famed zero-tolerance policy of trying minors as adults as often as possible.)

Proponents of trying minors as adults frequently cite weaknesses in the juvenile justice system, saying it is an insufficient deterrent for criminally-minded youths. And how, they add, can you justify to a murder victim's family a light sentence just because the person who killed their loved one was a kid?

Trying Juveniles as Adults Represents a Double Standard

Fair enough, but can we really justify a justice system in which a person can go to prison for life for something they did when they were 12 years-old? Do we really want to encourage cycles of poverty, poor education, and violence by throwing juvenile delinquents into jail with hardened adult criminals for decades at a time?

To be clear, I am not advocating leniency toward people who commit serious crimes. If a violent crime is committed, justice needs to be served no matter who the criminal—but "justice" means a proportional and appropriate punishment.

In other areas of the law minors are viewed as mentally incompetent, a caveat our justice system takes seriously when deliberating the guilt or innocence of adult criminals. Society (rightly, in my opinion) denies minors the right to vote, drink, independently sign legal contracts, run for office, adopt children, buy property, and so forth. It recognizes that our grasp of right and wrong is not fully developed for most of our minority, and thus establishes 18 as the legal age at which we are fully responsible for our choices.

Our grasp of right and wrong is not fully developed for most of our minority.

Trying minors as adults, therefore, represents a double standard in the legal system: a 15 year-old is too young and stupid to decide for himself whether cigarettes are something he should buy, but he is of sound adult mind when firing a gun in the midst of an argument.

Often in instances where minors are tried as adults, the crimes themselves are evidence of immaturity, not malice. Prosecutors frequently call violent crimes committed by minors "adult" in nature, but this confuses the severity of the crime and the maturity of criminal: whether a 12 year-old steals a candy bar or kills a man over it, his maturity level and mental competence hasn't changed. Rather the severity of the crime, and of the consequence, has changed. (Indeed, the trivial motives of many violent crimes committed by minors demonstrate this—such as Lionel Tate's attempt to practice a WWF [World Wrestling Federation] move on a 6 year-old.)

Adult Prisons Do More Harm than Good for Juveniles

All of this was acknowledged a century ago when the juvenile justice system came into existence. In 1899, at the height of the Progressive Era, the first Juvenile court opened in Chicago with the philosophy that rehabilitation, rather than punishment, should be the objective when dealing with juveniles. Reformers acknowledged that minors and adults had different rehabilitative needs and that before a certain age offenders are sufficiently impressionable that they can be "corrected" and safely reinserted in society. Juvenile detention centers were thus developed to place an emphasis on rewarding good behavior, instilling discipline, completing education, and reinsertion.

Rehabilitation, rather than punishment, should be the objective when dealing with juveniles.

Place this in contrast to adult prisons, and the differences are astounding. A recent report by the Center for Policy Alternatives reveals:

> Youths held in adult jails are eight times more likely to commit suicide, five times more likely to be sexually assaulted, twice as likely to be beaten by staff, and 50 percent more likely to be assaulted with a weapon than youth in juvenile facilities.

Moreover, minors sent to adult prisons are significantly more likely to reoffend, and twice as likely to be arrested for a more serious crime, than minors in the juvenile justice system.

Jailing minors alongside adult criminals makes them become more violent and less likely to be rehabilitated.

Extensive studies (and common sense) tell us that teenagers jailed alongside adult criminals become harder and *more* violent than those kept in juvenile detention. They are subject to "sentences" far harsher than those rendered by judges and juries, in the form of rape, physical abuse, torture, and suicide. Despite a Department of Justice report that nearly 40% of juveniles in adult prisons were convicted of nonviolent offenses, there is abundant evidence that jailing minors alongside adult criminals makes them become more violent and less likely to be rehabilitated.

And unsurprisingly, nearly 77% of minors in adult prisons represent a racial minority, primarily African American, while the vast majority hails from low-income families with poorly-educated parents.

Trying minors as adults represents a gross flaw in the current justice system. It draws the newest and least privileged members of society into horrific cycles of violence and depression, allowing them little path to rehabilitation, forgiveness, and productive lives. To address weaknesses in the juvenile justice system by simply bumping minors into adult courts and prisons disserves both minors and the adult prison system.

Moreover, how many of us would like to be held accountable, for the rest of our lives, for the decisions we made when we were 13? And how many of us rely on our education, our wealth, and the support of our families to keep us from making grave choices, and to protect us from disproportional harm? Each year thousands of American teenagers face years of abuse in violent adult prisons for crimes they committed without these benefits. Their crimes are horrific and punishable, but their punishments are not proportional. The practice of sending minors to adult courts represents a terrible and embarrassing double standard in the American legal system, and should be written out of law nationwide.

2

Juveniles Should Be Tried as Adults in Certain Circumstances

Mary Onelia Estudillo

Mary Onelia Estudillo has written several articles for The Guardian, *the student newspaper of the University of California at San Diego.*

The juvenile justice system was originally created to provide individualized rehabilitation to offenders of minor crimes such as truancy, shoplifting, and vandalism. But youth today are taking advantage of this lenient and outdated system and are committing violent crimes because they believe they will get off easy. In order to provide justice to victims and their families and to prevent more and more juveniles from committing violent crimes, the United States must hold criminals accountable—regardless of their age—and impose a tough punishment system. To that end, juveniles should sometimes be tried as adults.

It is not a war on youth. It is a battle against the immeasurable loss of human life, personal security and wasted human resources. When juvenile court preservationists label youth punishment initiatives as representative of moral bankruptcy and blame disinterested corporations and white, wealthy communities for disenfranchising the youth, people of color and the poor, they fail to put themselves in the position of the daughters whose Dartmouth parents were brutally

Mary Onelia Estudillo, "Paying Time for Committing Crime," *The Guardian*, February 27, 2001. Copyright © 2001 The Guardian. Reproduced by permission of The Guardian.

stabbed in the head and chest by 16- and 17-year-old boys. They forget the pain of the Columbine [high school in Colorado] shootings. They forget to put themselves in the shoes of a parent whose 5-year-old daughter was killed for her bike. They forget that a crime is a crime, regardless of the offender's age. They forget that sometimes, the criminal justice system works harder for the criminal than the victim.

Violent Youth Deserve Punishment

Now, don't get me wrong. I do not believe that institutionalization is a solution to America's social problems. I am a strong advocate of rehabilitation and second chances. There has been many a time in my life, as I'm sure there has been in everyone else's, that being given the second chance has made the difference. But I do believe, however trite this may sound, that if you do an adult crime, you do adult time. Minors that commit certain serious crimes should be tried as adults.

Some youths are even known to commit crimes without thought because they know they cannot be tried as adults.

Violent, preventable crimes by minors have long plagued America's larger cities but have scarcely been punished because of the age of the perpetrators. Protected by a lenient and highly outdated juvenile justice system, violent youth have taken advantage of such benefits and have run rampant in our cities. High profile slayings are quite the norm on the evening news, and every once in a while, disaster strikes and we lose a large number of lives at the hands of young offenders. And sadly, naive America continues to lose more and more lives at the hands of reckless teens and repeat offenders because we choose to give them as many chances as they need so long as they are not legal adults. Unfortunately, we have to lose and destroy more lives because we refuse to punish.

The Juvenile Justice System Cannot Keep Up

Many juvenile court sentences have amounted to nothing but a mere slap on the wrist for many young offenders. The juvenile court is no longer capable of providing the individualized attention that it first sought out to do and can no longer easily help at-risk offenders who are threats even after their juvenile sentences. Laws were first created to handle small cases such as truancy, shoplifting and vandalism. These laws are now archaic, as they do not have the ability to handle today's violent crimes. Tougher crimes call for tougher measures. Rehab centers have had little influence on youths. The counselors that deal with our youth are inexperienced and do not have the skills to counteract their behavior. For some violent youths, rehabilitation is the easy way out. Some youths are even known to commit crimes without thought because they know they cannot be tried as adults. Eventually, many young offenders who go through juvenile systems do not end up rehabilitated and, as a result, turn back to crime. In many jurisdictions, a child may have to commit 10 to 15 serious crimes before anything is actually done to him.

Without a tougher punishment system, society is left with a high percentage of delinquents and a rising percentage of crime victims.

Children are killed by children. Teens are killed by teens. And still we refuse to punish them because "they are too young to understand that what they are doing is wrong." An excuse most heard from parents, it is also an excuse too often heard after lives are lost and ruined. Without a tougher punishment system, society is left with a high percentage of delinquents and a rising percentage of crime victims.

Criminals Must Be Held Accountable

For many victims, the juvenile court systems have been a far cry from justice. Families of murder victims, rape targets and victims of other serious crimes have been left abandoned without a sense of closure, a sense of protection. Some feel like their loss was left unacknowledged. Indeed, in such a lenient juvenile system, victims are more often than not left unacknowledged. Most people agree with Sterling Burnett of the National Center for Policy Analysis in Dallas: "The only way to treat the victim as a full human being—to fully honor the memory of the victim—is to punish the perpetrator. . . ."

Minors must be fully culpable for their behavior if we are to deter future delinquents from committing violent crimes.

Trying minors as adults will toughen the system and hold someone responsible. Minors must be fully culpable for their behavior if we are to deter future delinquents from committing violent crimes. Setting this example and making it known that our cities will, indeed, be tough on crimes, will serve as a wake-up call. Like the three strikes law, the threat of a harsh sentence will most certainly make children think twice before they commit violent crimes.

Since 1993, at least 43 states have passed laws making it easier for children to be tried as adults. A juvenile justice bill is currently awaiting final Congressional approval and contains similar measures for the federal system. Proposition 21 [which stiffened penalties for juvenile offenders], from last year's [2000] California elections, was passed and, although it has stirred much opposition and controversy, it has molded the image that society will have no tolerance for crime. The cost of implementing such measures will never even reach the immeasurable cost of lives lost.

In the words of former California Gov. Pete Wilson we have to act "decisively to retake [our] neighborhoods. . . ." If we are to sincerely make an effort to keep our cities safer, all of America has to understand that youth may not be adults, but they are certainly capable of committing crimes. The crime that a 16-year-old commits is no different than that of a 60-year-old—thus, there should be no reason to treat them differently. Second chances will come accordingly, but accountability should come first. It is not about giving children second chances. It is about making them responsible for their actions.

3

The Death Penalty for Minors Should Be Considered on a Case-by-Case Basis

Dan Cutrer

Dan Cutrer, a Texas attorney, filed an amici curiae *brief on behalf of the victims' rights group Justice For All regarding the juvenile death penalty case* Roper v. Simmons, *before the United States Supreme Court.* Amici curiae, *which literally means "friends of the court," refers to professional people or organizations who volunteer to provide relevant information to the Court in deciding a matter before it.*

In 2004 the Supreme Court of the United States heard arguments to decide whether sentencing persons under the age of eighteen to the death penalty constitutes cruel and unusual punishment and should therefore be unconstitutional. However, the Court should not group all juvenile murderers into a single class; instead, juveniles should be given individual consideration and evaluated on their particular maturity level, intelligence, life experiences, and feelings of moral responsibility. Indeed, some juveniles—Christopher Simmons is an example—are fully capable of forming an intent to kill, understanding that murder is morally wrong, and carrying out the murder with no remorse. These unique individuals do deserve the death penalty.

Editor's note: On March 1, 2005, the U.S. Supreme Court decided that it is unconstitutional to impose the death penalty on persons who committed crimes while under the age of eighteen.

Dan Cutrer, Brief of *Amici Curiae* Justice For All Alliance in Support of Petitioner to the Supreme Court of the United States, *Donald P. Roper, Superintendent, Potosi Correctional Center, Petitioner v. Christopher Simmons, Respondent,* 2003.

The issue before the Court is whether the execution of a person who committed premeditated murder while under the age of eighteen constitutes "cruel and unusual punishment" in violation of the Eighth Amendment to the Constitution of the United States of America. . . .

The foundation of our judicial system is based on moral culpability. In intentional torts [wrongful acts] and criminal law the judicial system requires a requisite mental state in order to convict one of a crime. In criminal law, specifically murder cases, punishment is imposed according to one's degree of mens rea [criminal intent]. In fact, one of the rationales for imposing the death penalty, deterrence, is directly linked to one's moral culpability because the threat of death prevents one from forming the intent to kill. The ultimate penalty is imposed on those who intend to kill, understand right from wrong and the consequences of their actions at the time of the act and nevertheless kill another human being. Juveniles are capable of understanding right from wrong and the consequences of their actions. Furthermore, they are capable of forming the requisite intent to kill to merit the death penalty. They are also capable of being deterred from forming the requisite intent as will be illustrated in the analysis of the instant case.

The Court and a majority of state legislatures have held that individual consideration is a constitutional requirement before sentencing one to death. The Court needs to abide by this requirement and not group juveniles together as a class based on age. Rather, it should recognize that juvenile defendants, even those in the same age group, are shaped by individual life experiences and therefore possess different levels of maturity and make different choices. Consequently, their decisions affect their moral responsibility for a crime. . . .

Executing the Respondent [Christopher Simmons] is not cruel and unusual punishment because he specifically knew it was wrong to kill, understood the consequences of his actions, and nevertheless committed a horrific premeditated murder of an innocent woman. His justification for the murder was that he knew his age would prevent him from receiving the ultimate punishment. Juveniles like Simmons, need to be deterred from committing such an egregious act for the safety of society by being properly punished. The Respondent's execution furthers the goals of the death penalty because he deserves his life be taken as a result of him intentionally taking an innocent woman's life. Furthermore, it sends a message to other juveniles that when one understands the repercussions, knows right from wrong and still commits premeditated murder, he or she will receive the ultimate penalty. . . .

Intent to Kill Deserves the Death Penalty

The Court should consider whether respondent intended to kill. Respondent's intent to kill is evidenced by his statements to his friends that he would "find someone to burglarize, tie the victim up, and ultimately push the victim off the bridge." He planned to kill and in fact told his friends to meet him at a particular location at a particular time to commit murder. Furthermore, respondent deliberated over killing Mrs. [Shirley] Crook when he burglarized her home, taped her hands behind her back, taped her eyes and mouth shut, placed her in the back of the minivan and drove her from her house in Jefferson County [Missouri] to Castlewood State Park in St. Louis County. Respondent's actions—pulling her out of the van, restraining her hands and feet, covering her head with a towel, bounding her hands and feet together with electrical cable, hog-tie fashion, covering her face with electrical tape and then pushing her off the railroad trestle into the river— clearly reveal that he intended to kill her.

The next factor the Court should consider is whether respondent understood the consequences of his actions at the time he committed murder. The respondent understood the consequences of his actions evidenced by the fact he denied any knowledge of the crime because he knew if he told the truth he would serve either jail time or receive the ultimate penalty. His confession along with his statements to his friends showing his motive reveals that he knew and understood that robbing a woman and pushing her off the cliff would kill her. In fact, his belief that his age would allow him to "get away with it" shows a reckless indifference to human life and knowledge of the consequences of his actions.

If he knew that he would have received the ultimate punishment, he would have thought twice about committing murder and an innocent woman's life may have been saved.

Third, the Court should consider whether execution is proportional to the crime the respondent committed. Here, respondent committed a premeditated murder of an innocent woman by taking her out of her home to a park and pushing her off of a cliff when she was terribly afraid of heights. He intended to kill her and did so in a fashion disrespecting her humanity with no remorse. Respondent's execution furthers the goals of the death penalty because it gives him his just dessert and sends a message to other juveniles that if you understand the consequences of your actions and still commit premeditated murder, you will suffer the ultimate price.

Age Must Not Be an Excuse to Commit Murder

The Court should consider all relevant mitigating and aggravating factors. Here, the defense presented the following mitigating factors: respondent being seventeen and arguably unable to think about the future, vote or lawfully drink alcohol. The prosecution presented respondent's age as an aggravating factor implying that he could only get worse. The manner in which respondent killed Mrs. Crook along with his intent to kill are also aggravating factors. It seems that the aggravating circumstances outweigh the mitigating because of the atrociousness of the crime and respondent's moral culpability. Being seventeen years of age at the time of this murder did not prevent him from forming the requisite mental state to merit the death penalty. In fact, his perceived justification for killing Mrs. Crook was that he was going to "get away with it." If he knew that he would have received the ultimate punishment, he would have thought twice about committing murder and an innocent woman's life may have been saved. Punishment needs to be linked to respondent's moral culpability in a society that relies on the judicial system rather than self-help to vindicate their wrongs. Otherwise, people will feel a sense of injustice and rely on vigilante justice or lynch law.

The foundation of our judicial system is based on moral culpability. This Court has consistently held that punishment must be directly linked to one's blameworthiness. In fact, "causing harm intentionally must be punished more severely than causing the same harm unintentionally." One of the rationales for imposing the death penalty, deterrence, is linked to moral culpability because it is based on the notion that a person will not form the requisite intent to kill because of the threat of death. In the instant case, respondent likely would not have committed murder if he knew that he would have received the ultimate penalty.

The respondent would like this Court to wrongfully assume that he cannot think about the future nor possess the requisite mental state to merit the ultimate penalty because of his age and inability to vote or lawfully drink alcohol. However, it is evident by respondent's actions, confession, and statement to his friend that he would "get away with it" that he did possess the requisite mental state to merit the death penalty and further was able to rationalize that he would escape the consequences of his actions.

This Court acknowledged in *Tison v. Arizona*, that a societal consensus exists to impose the death penalty on one who did not kill nor intend to kill but was merely a major participant in a felony murder. The rationale for this decision was that actively participating in a felony murder shows a reckless disregard for human life; a highly culpable mental state meriting the death penalty.

Intending to kill and following through with that intention is a higher culpable mental state than participating in an act that shows a reckless disregard for human life. Therefore, society deems it acceptable to execute a seventeen-year-old who committed an act of murder, intended to kill and rationalized that he would escape the ultimate punishment for his actions because of his age.

This Court has consistently held that intentional harm must be punished more severely than unintentional harm. In *Tison*, the petitioner did not specifically intend to kill the victims nor did he kill them. In contrast, the respondent in the instant case had the specific intent to kill and did in fact kill the victim. In *Tison*, the petitioner was executed. Therefore, the respondent in the instant case should be executed.

The instant case exemplifies both the importance of the death penalty in society and the justification for its existence. In the instant case, the respondent was not deterred from committing murder because he knew his age would prevent him from receiving the ultimate punishment. This implies that had respondent known he would have received the ultimate penalty he would not have committed the act of murder.

Each juvenile defendant is different with respect to their maturity, intelligence, capabilities, life experiences, personal responsibility, and moral guilt.

This Court is being asked to draw a bright line rule at an arbitrary age of eighteen. The Court should not draw a bright line rule at the arbitrary age of eighteen because age does not define one's character, judgment, maturity, personal responsibility or moral guilt. In fact, drawing a bright line based on age "treats all persons convicted of a designated offense not as uniquely individual human beings, but as members of a faceless, undifferentiated mass." Furthermore, it violates a fundamental principle underlying the Eighth Amendment. Respect for humanity requires "consideration of the character and record of the individual offender and the circumstances of the particular offense" before deciding whether one merits the ultimate penalty.

Fifteen, sixteen, and seventeen-year-olds can possess the requisite mental state to merit the ultimate penalty.

This Court and a majority of state legislatures have held that individual consideration is a constitutional requirement before sentencing one to death. This Court needs to abide by this precedent and not group juveniles together as a class but rather recognize that each juvenile defendant is different with respect to their maturity, intelligence, capabilities, life experiences, personal responsibility, and moral guilt. This Court should uphold Justice [Sandra Day] O'Connor's ruling in *Thompson [v. Oklahoma]* [1988] in which she stated "granting the premise that adolescents are generally less blameworthy than adults who commit similar crimes, it does not necessarily follow that all fifteen-year-olds [who murder] are incapable of the moral culpability that would justify the imposition of capital punishment." Juveniles can form the requisite intent to kill, and are able to both understand the consequences of their actions and conform their conduct to civilized standards. In fact, juveniles are mature enough to understand and know that murdering another person is wrong.

Juvenile Murderers Need Individual Consideration

Fifteen, sixteen, and seventeen-year-olds can possess the requisite mental state to merit the ultimate penalty. However, it is essential to look at the merits of each individual case as a constitutional requirement. In *Thompson v. Oklahoma*, a fifteen-year-old brutally murdered his brother in law. The petitioner shot his brother in law twice, cut his throat, chest, abdomen, and broke his leg. Thereafter, he chained the body to a concrete block and threw it into a river where it remained for approximately four weeks. In *Wilkins v. Missouri*, a sixteen-year-old planned to rob a store and "murder whoever was behind the counter because a dead person can't talk." Wilkins carried out his plan by stabbing a victim a total of eight times. The victim was stabbed once causing him to fall and then three times in the chest, and four more times in the neck after pleading for his life. Wilkins left the scene, leaving the victim to die on the floor. In *Stanford v. Kentucky*, a seventeen-year-old repeatedly raped and sodomized a victim during and after the commission of a robbery at a gas station where the victim had worked. The victim was driven to a secluded area where Stanford shot her in the face and in the back of her head. Stanford knew the victim and killed her because he was afraid she would identify him. In all of the three cases mentioned above, each petitioner knew what he was doing, each intended to kill, and each made the conscious decision to follow through with his intention, showing no remorse. Ultimately, each one possessed the requisite moral culpability to merit the death penalty irrespective of their age. . . .

Instead of grouping juveniles together as a class and drawing a bright line rule based on age, this Court should look at juveniles individually and respect them as human beings with unique characteristics, life experiences, personal responsibility and moral blameworthiness. . . .

Furthermore, this Court should require the states that authorize capital punishment to apply it on a case-by-case basis focusing on the individual's moral culpability. It is unthinkable to follow any other course in a judicial system that relies on precedent and fixed rules of law. By applying the proposed standard, the Court respects a person's pride and dignity whose life has been shattered as a result of one's selfish decision to kill.

4

The Death Penalty Should Never Be Considered for Minors

Drew S. Days III

Drew S. Days III is the counsel of record who filed the amici curiae *brief on behalf of the American Psychological Association and the Missouri Psychological Association regarding the juvenile death penalty case* Roper v. Simmons *before the U.S. Supreme Court.*

Because of their immaturity, juveniles should never be subject to the death penalty. The frontal lobes of adolescents' brains, which affect their ability to control impulses and to anticipate the consequences of their actions, have not yet reached adult maturity. Logically, it should follow that this diminished capacity also diminishes a juvenile's blameworthiness when committing a capital offense. Even when evaluated on an individual basis, the character of a juvenile has not fully developed, and it is therefore impossible to predict any future criminal behavior. Adolescent immaturity also undermines the ability of juveniles to make knowledgeable decisions in their defense to the extent that they sometimes give false confessions, resulting in wrongful convictions and executions. For these and other reasons, the death penalty should never be considered for minors.

Drew S. Days III, Brief for the American Psychological Association, and the Missouri Psychological Association as *Amici Curiae* Supporting Respondent, to the Supreme Court of the United States, *Donald P. Roper, Superintendent, Potosi Correctional Center, Petitioner v. Christopher Simmons, Respondent*, July 19, 2004.

Editor's Note: On March 1, 2005, the Supreme Court of the United States decided that it is unconstitutional to impose the death penalty on persons committing crimes while under the age of eighteen.

At ages 16 and 17, adolescents, as a group, are not yet mature in ways that affect their decision-making. Behavioral studies show that late adolescents are less likely to consider alternative courses of action, understand the perspective of others, and restrain impulses. Delinquent, even criminal, behavior is characteristic of many adolescents, often peaking around age 18. Heightened risk-taking is also common. During the same period, the brain has not reached adult maturity, particularly in the frontal lobes, which control executive functions of the brain related to decision-making.

Adolescents often lack an adult ability to control impulses and anticipate the consequences of their actions.

Adolescent risk-taking often represents a tentative expression of adolescent identity and not an enduring mark of behavior arising from a fully formed personality. Most delinquent adolescents do not engage in violent illegal conduct through adulthood.

The unformed nature of adolescent character makes execution of 16- and 17-year-olds fall short of the purposes this Court has articulated for capital punishment. Developmentally immature decision-making, paralleled by immature neurological development, diminishes an adolescent's blameworthiness. With regard to deterrence, adolescents often lack an adult ability to control impulses and anticipate the consequences of their actions. Studies call into question the effect on juvenile recidivism [repeat criminal behavior] of harsher criminal sanctions.

Evaluation of Future Moral Character Is Impossible

The mitigating effect of adolescence cannot be reliably assessed in individualized capital sentencing. Adolescents are "moving targets" for assessment of character and future dangerousness, two important considerations in the penalty phase of capital trials. As one example, psychologists have been unable to identify chronic psychopathy, also known as sociopathy, among adolescents. Assessments of such severe antisocial behaviors during adolescence have yet to be shown to remain stable as individuals grow into adulthood. Consequently, attempts to predict at capital sentencing an adolescent offender's character formation and dangerousness in adulthood are inherently prone to error and create an obvious risk of wrongful execution.

The transitory nature of adolescence also means that an adolescent defendant is much more likely to change in relevant respects between the time of the offense and the time of assessment by courts and experts. At sentencing, an offender may behave and look more like an adult than he or she did at the time the crime was committed. Impressions of the maturity and responsibility of adolescent offenders may also be impermissibly influenced by unconscious racism.

Immaturity of judgment, which is generally characteristic of adolescent development, will affect a defendant's participation in earlier stages of the criminal process. A recent study found adolescents overrepresented among defendants who had falsely confessed to crimes. Other research that examined psychosocial influences on legal decisions found that developmental immaturity may adversely affect an adolescent's decisions, attitudes, and behavior in the role of defendant. Individualized capital sentencing cannot correct for the heightened risk of error produced by less mature adolescent decision-making at earlier stages of the criminal process. . . .

The likelihood of error in ascertaining putatively [supposed] enduring features of an adolescent's behavior is high. The fundamental problem is found in the inability to distinguish in a reliable way between the few adolescent offenders who may not be amenable to rehabilitation and the many who will spontaneously desist or who will respond to sanction or intervention. The absence of proof that assessments of adolescent behavior will remain stable into adulthood invites unreliable capital sentencing based on faulty appraisals of character and future conduct. . . .

Appearance Matures Between the Crime and the Sentencing

Even if a sufficiently reliable means existed to assess the true character and future dangerousness of an adolescent defendant, the maturation of an adolescent that occurs between the date of a crime and the time of a capital sentencing assessment further complicates efforts to capture accurately an adolescent's capacities and maturity at the time of an offense. The lapse in time is likely to involve much more significant psychological changes in adolescents than in adults.

Having advanced further through puberty, the defendant may have more the appearance of a man than the boy who committed the offense.

An evaluation performed for the purpose of capital sentencing will consider an adolescent who has, necessarily, aged since the date of the offense. Having advanced further through puberty, the defendant may have more the appearance of a man than the boy who committed the offense. In one juvenile case, jurors imposed a death sentence, at least in part, based on the defendant's seemingly adult physical appearance.

The defendant was nearing 21 years of age by the time of trial, was physically imposing, unusually tall, and characterized by one juror as a "tall, pretty muscular black guy." Interestingly, several jurors described him "as utterly emotionless, despite other jurors' reports of his tears at the mention of his murdered brother" and his mother's testimony.

Neurodevelopmental maturation may have altered the adolescent's impulsivity, difficulty in weighing options, vulnerabilities to situational factors or other features of relative developmental immaturity that existed at the time of the offense. Exposure to the adult corrections system while awaiting trial and sentencing can also affect adolescents, their behavior and their presentation. In a study of the impact of incarceration on adolescents, offenders reported that, at best, experience in adult facilities was a test of will and endurance and, at worst, a painful and denigrating experience that served as reason to become "more angry, embittered, cynical and defeated." . . .

A stereotyped belief that African American adolescents possess more adult-like criminal intent may taint judgments about the culpability of adolescent offenders.

A more adult appearance at sentencing is harder to reconcile with whatever mitigating evidence of immaturity may be introduced. The professional opinion rendered by experts for the purpose of capital sentencing and the impression left with the sentencer during trial will reflect an older, more mature person, even though the offending behaviors at issue were adolescent. Thus, in many cases, the judge and jury will encounter a person who is different in highly relevant respects from the individual who committed the crime. The passage of months or perhaps years between the offense and sentencing may punish a defendant because he appears, thinks, and behaves in a more mature fashion than he did when he committed the offense, eliminating the opportunity to judge the defendant's developmental state at the time of the crime. . . .

Unconscious Racism Affects Judgement

The assessment of the maturity and responsibility of individual adolescent offenders also can be impermissibly influenced by unconscious bias. Recent research has revealed that a stereotyped belief that African American adolescents possess more adult-like criminal intent may taint judgements about the culpability of adolescent offenders. Police officers and probation officers reported more negative trait ratings, greater perceived culpability, less child-like qualities and recommended harsher punishment for adolescents after the officers were provided a set of subliminal cues related to African Americans.

The possibility of false confessions ... increase[s] ... the likelihood that adolescents will be convicted, and then executed, in error.

Police and probation officers induced to think about African Americans were less likely to judge the hypothetical juvenile offenders as immature, and more likely to think of them as adult-like in their behavior.

Previous research found that probation officers are more likely to attribute the criminality of African American adolescents to negative personal defects such as a lack of remorse, while they are more likely to attribute criminal behavior of white adolescents to negative environmental causes such as a dysfunctional family. . . .

Immature Decision-Making Adversely Affects Trials

Judgments made by adolescents, who on average are less mature than adults, will also affect a defendant's participation at the stages of the criminal process before sentencing. Adolescent immaturity undermines a defendant's ability to make meaningful and fully informed decisions to manage his or her own defense. Decisions by a defendant throughout the investigatory and trial process may influence whether the death penalty will be sought or imposed. As is true for defendants with mental retardation, the possibility of false confessions, difficulties in giving meaningful assistance to counsel, and poor performance as witnesses all increase the likelihood that adolescents will be convicted, and then executed, in error.

A recent analysis found that adolescents were over-represented among those who falsely confessed in response to interrogation. Among a total of 113 false confessors, 16% were between the ages of 16 and 17, representing the highest concentration among any averaged two-year age group. Among all cases studied, false confessions were concentrated in the most serious offenses, the overwhelming majority occurring in murder cases (81%), followed by cases of rape (9%) and arson (3%). One case was that of the Central Park jogger victim in which four 14- to 16-year-old defendants were convicted of rape or other crimes on the basis of their confessions, but later were exonerated by DNA evidence linking the crime to a notorious serial rapist.

False evidence presented by authorities to an individual in an effort to elicit a confession can lead an individual to confess to an act he or she did not commit. The same individual may then internalize the confession and confabulate details consistent with the false confession. . . . Research indicates that adolescents are more susceptible to these kinds of suggestions of guilt than are adults. In a study comparing 15- and 16-year-olds to young adults ages 18 to 26, the adolescents were more likely to take responsibility for a mock crime when presented with false evidence of their guilt.

The reliability of convictions and sentences can also be directly affected by adolescent defendants' understanding of their legal rights. In a recent study of more than 1,300 adolescents and young adults, researchers found adolescent immaturity of judgment reflected in adolescent decision-making concerning criminal proceedings.

The research examined psychosocial influences on legal decisions that criminal defendants are often required to make, involving whether to confess to the police or remain silent, whether or to what extent to communicate with counsel, and whether to accept a prosecutor's plea offer. After participants completed a standardized measure of abilities relevant to competency to stand trial, *i.e.*, participating in and understanding the trial process, researchers went on to assess the relationship between immaturity and the choices made in the course of a criminal adjudication. Adolescents, including older adolescents who scored at adult levels on measures of capacity relevant to legal competence to stand trial, nonetheless tended more often than adults to make choices that reflected the influences of psychosocial immaturity.

Although older adolescents were more likely than younger adolescents to recognize potential risks and understand how unpleasant consequences would be if they occurred, their perception of the likelihood that the adverse consequences would actually occur was not significantly different than that of younger adolescents. Consequently, the researchers concluded that "psychosocial immaturity may affect a young person's decisions, attitudes, and behavior in the role of defendant in ways that do not directly implicate competence to stand trial, but that may be quite important to how they make choices, interact with police, relate to their attorneys, and respond to the trial context." That means that adolescents "may make different legal decisions than they themselves would make in their adult years."

5

Life Without Parole Should Be Prohibited for Minors

Ari Paul

Ari Paul is a reporter for the Chief-Leader, *a weekly newspaper covering municipal labor unions in New York City. He also has written articles that have appeared in many other publications.*

Despite the fact that the United Nations' Convention on the Rights of the Child declares that juvenile criminals never deserve sentences of life without parole, the United States continues to sanction that harsh punishment. Beginning in the 1980s, when national homicide rates soared, the American political culture adopted a tough-on-crime attitude, and by the late 1990s most states were trying juveniles as adults. Finally, however, America appears to be leaning toward reforming the juvenile justice system so that children will be treated with more concern. As an example, California state senator Leland Yee has introduced the Juvenile Life Without Parole Reform Act, which emphasizes rehabilitation for minors rather than punishment.

There can only be a few issues where government policies in countries like Libya and Burma appear more progressive than those in the United States. Juvenile sentencing is one of them.

The United States currently imprisons 2,270 people who have life sentences without the chance for parole for crimes

Ari Paul, "America's Imprisoned Kids: The United States Is an Outlier in the World When it Comes to Detaining and Sentencing Juvenile Offenders as Adults. But There Are Finally Signs of Change," *Prospect.org*, May 11, 2007. Copyright © 2007 The American Prospect, 11 Beacon Street, Suite 1120, Boston, MA 02108.

they committed when they were minors, according to both Human Rights Watch [HRW] and Amnesty International; in all other nations on Earth, there are a combined total of only 12 such prisoners, HRW says. These are grim figures to prison reform advocates in the United States, who have long battled with the punitive, get-tough ethos that dominates American political discussion about criminal justice issues. But there are notable signs of a turn in the political winds.

America Is Tougher than Other Countries on Juvenile Offenders

Alison Parker, a researcher for HRW, has documented this kind of sentencing, and the United States is far behind the curve when it comes to the rights of child prisoners. The United Nations' Convention on the Rights of the Child [CRC] provides that children may not receive life sentences without parole or the death penalty. All member states have ratified the CRC—except Somalia and the United States. (Both have signed the treaty but have not ratified it.)

African American criminal youths in California receive life without parole at a rate 22 times that for their white counterparts.

The reality, she maintains, is that most countries do not even contemplate sanctioning this kind of punishment. (This isn't to say that the rest of the world is perfect on the matter. "Israel, South Africa and Tanzania reported that they were in violation of the treaty," Parker says.) Domestically, what is just as disturbing for Parker is that her research has found that African American criminal youths in California receive life without parole at a rate 22 times that for their white counterparts.

For Babe Howell, a law professor at New York University and a former criminal defense attorney, this is a symptom of something larger in the United States. "I think we are so punitive in terms of juvenile sentencing for the same reasons why we are so punitive in terms of all other sentencing," she says. "The reason why we are so punitive otherwise is the harder question, although I think it may have to do with how diverse our society is and that criminal sentences generally fall on people regarded as 'other.' I also think that politics have a lot to do with it. Being soft on crime is untenable and voting for sentencing increases is just so easy."

The human brain is still maturing during adolescence, and therefore minors are more likely to rehabilitate.

Indeed, the trend in trying juveniles as adults started in earnest in the 1980s, when homicide rates in the nation started to soar. (Those rates have come down dramatically since.) By the late 1990s most states had made reforms to make the trial of juveniles as adults easier. And it was at this time that Senator Orrin Hatch of Utah introduced the get-tough Violent and Repeat Juvenile Offender Act, which passed in 1999.

The culture of excessive punishment pervades all parts of the American political spectrum.

The Political Attitude Is Changing

But there are some signs of a potential shift in that prevailing political culture. To take one of the most notable examples, a bill in the California Senate that would make it impossible for the state's judges to sentence criminals younger than 18 to life without the chance of parole is now [in May 2007] moving forward. In April 2007 the California Senate Committee on Public Safety passed the Juvenile Life Without Parole Reform Act. The state senator behind it is Leland Yee, a Democrat who has a doctorate in child psychology. He says that the human brain is still maturing during adolescence, and therefore minors are more likely to rehabilitate. "We should always sentence kids a little differently," says Adam Keigwin, a spokesperson for Sen. Yee.

A vote before the full state Senate should take place by mid-May [2007]. Some of the bill's supporters are hopeful about its eventual passage. In fact, Republican Governor Arnold Schwarzenegger has made at least some efforts to refocus the state's prison system towards rehabilitation. But Keigwin knows the supporters have to win over conservatives in the legislature, especially those allied with the Christian right. "The message of redemption is very important to them," Parker says. Meanwhile, to appeal to fiscally conservative lawmakers, Yee and the bill's supporters are arguing that it will cost the state $500 million to imprison the current population of minors sentenced without the chance of parole until their deaths.

But it remains the case that any such attempt to reform aspects of America's prison-industrial complex will involve tussling with powerful and entrenched interests. Moreover, the culture of executive punishment pervades all parts of the American political spectrum.

For example, while the Supreme Court, in the 2005 case *Roper v. Simmons*, ended by a vote of 5-4 the practice of putting to death inmates for crimes committed when they were minors, the written dissents are telling. Sandra Day O'Connor, then the court's famed moderate, said that a difference in maturity levels was not a compelling enough reason to rob the state's ability of executing such convicts. Antonin Scalia scoffed at the majority opinion's comparison to what other countries do. "'Acknowledgement' of foreign approval has no place in the legal opinion of this Court," he wrote. Rhetoric like that is an attempt to neuter the ability of attorneys to use an international standard in charging that specific punishments are 'cruel and unusual' and thus unconstitutional.

While many are hopeful about Yee's proposed legislation in California, if it too fails to pass, it will serve as an all-too-typical illustration of the shame that is America's sentencing policy.

"Given current politics it is not clear to me that there are any promising arguments against these sentencing norms but human rights law," says Howell. "International embarrassment may someday put us in a position where life sentences for juveniles become as embarrassing as Jim Crow [laws that mandated separate facilities for white and black people] did in the 1950s and 1960s."

6

Life Without Parole Should Not Be Prohibited for Minors

Trench Reynolds

Trench Reynolds is a North Carolina–based blogger who has been writing about school shootings and other juvenile-related crimes since 2000.

Most juveniles understand the difference between right and wrong and that murder is definitely wrong. So instead of being excused because of difficult childhoods or immaturity, juvenile offenders must be held accountable for their actions. When a person—regardless of age—commits murder under special circumstances, a judge needs to have the option of sentencing life without parole. That punishment not only acts as a deterrent for other juvenile offenders, but also provides justice for the victims. Juveniles must not be allowed to get away with murder.

As most of you know I write about juvenile offenders on an almost daily basis. Not only have I written about school shootings but I've also written about such teenage murderers as Patrick Armstrong, Scott Dyleski, the Zarate brothers, and Esmie Tseng. So I like to think I have a little bit of knowledge on the subject.

I am of the opinion that most juvenile offenders know the difference between right and wrong and that most know that murder is wrong. That being said I have no problem whatsoever with teenage killers being tried as adults and being subject to adult sentences.

Trench Reynolds, "Murder Is Never Juvenile," *www.crime.ws*, February 28, 2007. Reproduced by permission. http://thetrenchcoat.com/archives/2942-Murder-is-never-juvenile.html.

In California [in 1990] voters approved a law known as Proposition 115 which allows judges to sentence 16-year-olds who have committed murder with "special circumstances" . . . to life in prison without the possibility of parole. The most infamous teen killer to receive that sentence was the aforementioned Scott Dyleski.

Some Juveniles Deserve Life Without Parole

Scott Dyleski was tried and found guilty in the brutal slaying of Pam Vitale, the wife of famed criminal defense attorney Daniel Horowitz. Dyleski was 16 when he bludgeoned Pam Vitale to death with a piece of crown molding that he beat her with 39 times before carving a cross into her back. He was sentenced to life in prison without the possibility of parole.

Rehabilitation in adults or teens is the exception rather than the norm.

Now [2007] a California politician, Assemblyman Leland Yee, D-San Francisco, who also has a doctorate in child psychology, wants to repeal Proposition 115. He has proposed The California Juvenile Life Without Parole Reform Act which would block judges from sentencing minors to life without parole. Under the proposed legislation the most a teenage killer could receive is 25 years with parole. Yee believes that youthful offenders have the best chance of being rehabilitated.

Unfortunately teens are more capable of killing than ever before.

I've been doing this long enough that I've heard all the arguments. It's always the same old buzz words and phrases. Rehabilitation, they're not mature enough to understand their actions, they had hard childhoods, jail is not a deterrent. The Helen Lovejoys [a character from the animated television comedy *The Simpsons*] of the world who are always bemoaning "*Won't someone please think of the children?*" never use the following words. Punishment, personal responsibility, or justice for the victim. They're more concerned for the quality of life of the killer rather than the victim who has no life anymore. In my opinion rehabilitation in adults or teens is the exception rather than the norm. Proponents of this bill also claim it would help alleviate the prison population. Do you know what would be a surefire way to alleviate the prison population? If people stopped killing each other. So just because the prisons are crowded we're supposed to lessen the burden on the killers? Logic like that would make Aristotle roll in his grave. Not only that [but] teens are not as stupid as supporters of this new legislation make them out to be. Who do you go to when you can't work a feature on your cell phone or computer? Especially with the degradation of parenting in our society teens are rushed into adulthood faster than ever.

Life Without Parole Is a Necessary Deterrent

Repealing Proposition 115 would be devastating in a state like California where gang violence is the most active in the country. All they would have to do is have their under 18 members carry out their killings so they'll have shorter sentences if they get caught. California has also had its share of school shootings such as the [2001] Santana High School shooting [in San Diego County in which two were killed and thirteen wounded]. Again if Prop 115 was repealed school shooters like [Santana's] Andy Williams would have no deterrent whatsoever from creating another Columbine [Colorado high school shooting in 1999 in which fifteen died and twenty-three were wounded].

This isn't the 1950's anymore where the worst thing juveniles did was graffiti, shoplifting, or smoking. This is the 21st

Century where unfortunately teens are more capable [of] killing than ever before. And I know this is cliche but I wonder how many supporters of The California Juvenile Life Without Parole Reform Act would still be supporters if one of their family [members] were the victim of the teen murderer.

Justice is supposed to be for the victim not for the condemned.

7

Adult Sentencing Does Not Deter Juveniles from Crime

Enrico Pagnanelli

Enrico Pagnanelli is a member of the editorial staff of the American Criminal Law Review, *which is published by the students of the Georgetown University Law Center.*

Due to a rise in the juvenile crime rate between 1985 and 1994, many Americans believed that the juvenile justice system had failed. As a result, the Juvenile Justice and Delinquency Prevention Act of 2002 was passed to increase the punishment for violent juvenile offenders and thereby protect the public. To that end, most states adopted policies that transfer juveniles to the adult criminal court system. Several studies, however, have shown that the adult criminal system has a significant negative impact on juveniles by obstructing any future educational, employment, and social opportunities. Furthermore, these studies also show that transferring juveniles does not deter them from re-offending, but actually encourages future criminal activity.

There is a clear consensus among scholars that public concern, particularly for violent crime, was a major factor contributing to the growing trend of transferring juveniles to the adult court system during the 1990's. Research has shown that the perception by adults of juvenile crime during this period was highly and systematically distorted in favor of over-construing the degree of serious juvenile offenses. Franklin

American Criminal Law Review, v. 44, Winter, 2007 for "Children as Adults: The Transfer of Juveniles to Adult Courts and the Potential Impact of *Roper v. Simmons*," by Enrico Pagnanelli. Copyright © 2007 Georgetown University Law Center. Reproduced by permission of the author.

Zimring, a leading scholar in juvenile crime, detects that there is a general sentiment that the youth population has an unusually high share of violent offenders, and consequently there has been a focus on preventing the potential violent crimes of this grown up demographic.

Misguided Public Opinion Led to Harsh Punishment for Juveniles

While there was an increase in violent juvenile crime during the period from 1985–1994, recent trends show that the "rate of juvenile violent crime arrests has consistently decreased since 1994, falling to a level not seen since at least the 1970s." Despite the decrease and plateau of violent crime, the hysteria from the 1985–1994 increase in juvenile crime created the perception of a crime wave. Violent crime among juveniles was one of the most hotly discussed topics in the 1990s. The majority who pushed for harsher policies believed the rehabilitative efforts of the juvenile system had failed. Media coverage of high profile crimes, as well as an overall distortion of seriousness of violent juvenile crimes, only contributed to this negative stigma towards the effectiveness of the juvenile justice system. Consequently, most Americans believed that juveniles should be treated with the same severity as adults, and this in turn led to pressure on legislatures to create laws that provide for transfer to the criminal court system, as well as other procedural mechanisms that treated violent juvenile offenders as adults.

Such pressure resulted in the passing of the Juvenile Justice and Delinquency Prevention Act of 2002 (hereinafter, Juvenile Act). The Juvenile Act sought to increase the accountability of violent juvenile offenders and even mentioned that penalties imposed by the juvenile system were unsuccessful. The clear purpose of the law was to address violent juvenile offenders in a more punitive manner resembling the adult court system. Many state legislatures had already responded "punitively to the youth violence epidemic of the mid 1980s to mid 1990s, and all but six states either expanded or implemented laws that sought to increase the number of juvenile offenders waived to adult criminal court." The Juvenile Act merely represents the federal codification of this trend, enshrining a national shift from a rehabilitative focus on juvenile crime to a new retributive focus on the treatment of violent juvenile offenders in American courts and legislatures. . . .

Studies show that transfer [to adult court] fails to deter violent juvenile offenders.

The crackdown on violent juvenile crimes and the invasion of retributive ideals into the juvenile justice system has created a multitude of judicial processes that have exponentially increased the transfer of juveniles to the criminal court system. What follows is a review of some compelling statistics on the breadth of juvenile transfer. Through the 2004 legislative session, forty-six states have judicial waiver provisions under which juvenile court judges may waive jurisdiction over individual juveniles, allowing criminal court prosecutions to take place. In forty-five states the waiver decision is left entirely to the judge's discretion, in fifteen states there is a rebuttable presumption in favor of waiver, and in fifteen states a mandatory waiver is provided under certain circumstances. Fifteen states authorize the prosecutor to decide whether to file certain kinds of cases in juvenile or criminal court. Twenty-nine states have "laws that exclude certain kinds of cases from the jurisdiction of the juvenile court and required they be tried in criminal court." In addition, thirty-four states have some variation of a once-an-adult-always-an-adult statute, twenty states either "authorize or mandate criminal prosecution of juveniles accused of drug offenses," and twenty-two states even "require or allow criminal prosecution of juveniles accused of certain property offenses."

Transferring Juveniles to Adult Courts Leads to Re-Offending

Studies show that transfer fails to deter violent juvenile offenders. In fact, various studies have indicated that transfer actually increases recidivism [repeat offending] among these offenders. This increased recidivism manifests a failure to deter, a failure to rehabilitate, and most significantly, a failure to protect society.

> *The transfer of violent juvenile offenders only increases their likelihood of re-offending.*

In his study, Jeffrey Fagan [Columbia Law School faculty author] examined the recidivism rates of fifteen and sixteen-year-olds charged with robbery. He compared the recidivism rate of such youths charged in criminal court under New York's automatic transfer statute to those charged in New Jersey's juvenile court and found a significant increase in the recidivism of juveniles who had been transferred to the adult system. Another study, analyzing recidivism rates among 2,738 juvenile offenders in Florida, found that recidivism was more likely and more severe for juveniles transferred to criminal courts. Similarly, a study in Minnesota found higher recidivism over a two-year period among juveniles who had been waived to adult court when compared to those who had stayed within the juvenile system. Arguably, the transfer of violent juvenile offenders only increases their likelihood of re-offending and has thus failed the inherent objective of transfer: protecting the public.

Transfer has a significant negative effect on a juvenile's development and may, therefore, be a direct cause of increased recidivism among transferred violent juvenile offenders relative to their counterparts in the juvenile system. Instead of rehabilitating, the criminal system may encourage recidivism. Juveniles who are incarcerated are more likely to "learn social rules and norms that legitimate domination, exploitation, and retaliation" from the surrounding adult criminals. The criminal system also may cause juveniles to feel exploited and humiliated by the judicial process, and stigmatized by society. A criminal conviction may also encourage recidivism by severely obstructing the convicted juvenile's future educational, employment, and social opportunities.

The juvenile court system is the most appropriate forum for juvenile offenders.

A juvenile who has been tried in a criminal court often feels unjustly treated, and juveniles with this negative perception of the adjudication process are more likely to adopt a "delinquent self-concept" which also causes them to re-offend. Extensive interviews with juvenile offenders in the adult criminal system reveal that they view the system as "duplicitous and manipulative, malevolent in intent, and indifferent to their needs." These reactions are wholly "inconsistent with compliance to legal norms," and highlight a very potent negative effect on incarcerated juveniles which logically contributes to increased rates of recidivism post-transfer.

Juvenile Offenders Belong in the Juvenile System

Transfer may have a very minimal deterrent effect on juveniles because their premature psychological development may prevent them from feeling culpability. Most juveniles do not perceive risks or appreciate the consequences of their actions the way adults do. While research is mixed on whether juveniles contain the necessary level of blameworthiness for culpability, the idea that juveniles may lack culpability because of psychological development is helpful in assessing whether transfer is appropriate. This evidence argues against any mandatory sentencing policy that fails at least to consider mitigating factors such as age, crime, and the capacity of blameworthiness for a juvenile offender.

The juvenile court system has many positive characteristics that help rehabilitate young offenders and reduce recidivism. Many young offenders who engage in chronic delinquency often fail to develop the relationships and attachments crucial to the process of socialization. Juveniles in the juvenile system are able to develop positive relationships with individuals involved in their care, such as judges, practitioners, and case workers. These relationships, in conjunction with the nurturing of the juvenile system's rehabilitation process stimulate the development of trust, core values, and character in juveniles and aid their effective reintegration into society.

One could argue that because a child has the legal right to many "adult decisions," treating juveniles as adults makes sense. However, this argument is a fatal misconstruction. That juveniles now enjoy some of the legal rights enjoyed by adults has no bearing on a juvenile's capacity to stand trial. The utilitarian goals of our justice system should not be ignored. The experience of childhood is necessary to socialize juveniles. It is essential that a justice system recognize this and cater to the many social and psychological deficits in the lives of juvenile offenders. Because of the negative effects of transfer, including increased post-transfer recidivism, and the juvenile system's focus on nurturing and re-socialization, the juvenile court system is the most appropriate forum for juvenile offenders—even violent offenders—and, ultimately, the most effective means of protecting the public.

8

Rehabilitation Deters Juveniles from Crime Better than Adult Prisons Do

Daniel B. Wood

Daniel B. Wood is a staff writer for the Christian Science Monitor.

After years of imposing a get-tough attitude toward juvenile criminals, the state of California has become frustrated that the system has failed to deter juveniles from committing crimes. As a result, state officials want to try a new approach and focus on rehabilitating youth instead of punishing them. Juvenile justice experts believe that individualized treatment, education, and life-preparation programs will have a positive impact on youth so that they will return to their community as productive citizens. Other states, including Missouri, Maryland, and Colorado, are also embracing rehabilitation over punishment despite obstacles such as funding and a fear of becoming too soft on crime.

After decades of tough policies, America's most-populous state is poised to reverse direction in its approach to the incarceration of youth—from punishment to rehabilitation.

In the 1930s and 1940s, in particular, California was considered the country's premier model for returning young offenders to communities only after addressing the shortcomings that may have led to their prison terms—social and education skills, family patterns, mental health, gang participation, and vocational needs.

Daniel B. Wood, "California Turns Toward Rehabilitating Juveniles," *The Christian Science Monitor*, May 27, 2005. Reproduced by permission from *Christian Science Monitor, (www.csmonitor.com)*.

But dwindling funds and years of embracing a get-tough ethos moved the state into what critics called the "caged" model: one more intent on control, rebuke, and reprimand than on corrective measures.

A New Approach to Juvenile Crime

Now [2005] with 70 percent of released offenders rearrested within three years—highlighting both the costs to society and declining life options for the imprisoned—the state is embracing a new approach. Goaded in part by a taxpayer lawsuit forcing them to address deficiencies, state leaders are releasing blueprints that they hope will stop the revolving door of juvenile offenders turning into adult criminals.

"We are not talking about hugging a thug . . . we will still hold youth accountable for what they do, but we need to make an impact on the majority of offenders so they don't go out there and reoffend," says Walt Allen, director of the California Youth Authority (CYA), which runs the state's eight youth prison facilities, now housing about 3,288 people.

[The state government in] Sacramento's move mirrors a trend underway in several states. In Missouri, for instance, youth offenders are housed in small facilities and given intensive treatment, training, and education. Maryland and other states are looking to revamp their programs, too.

An Emphasis on Rehabilitation

But the emerging California model would mark a move into rehabilitation on a scale not yet tried, state officials say. The hope is the system will help turn around one of the nation's most troubled juvenile-justice systems. Though funding for the initiative remains uncertain, the governor and state legislature are at least in agreement on philosophy: group therapy, self-discipline, and life-preparation programs are the antidote for recidivism—and cheaper in the long run.

As laid out in plans submitted in court documents last week, the CYA wants to move to smaller living units, increased staff-to-youth ratios, systematic assessment of juveniles, and individualized treatment. In addition, authorities want to change an environment that over the years has spilled into dangerous—and regular—fighting between wards and staff.

States are reframing their objectives with the premise that all these young criminal offenders end up back in local communities.

Paramount in that culture shift will be producing living conditions and rules that promote more appropriate behavior, reward the achievement of goals, and spell out sanctions for misbehaving. Such changes go beyond simple redefinitions of housing, staff, and the actual content of programs: They will try to shape the way prisoners interact—which might carry over to nonprison life.

"The lawsuit and our subsequent investigation of what is working well in other states made us realize that what we need is a much more large-scale overhaul," says Elizabeth Siggins, assistant secretary for juvenile justice policy.

In addition to Missouri, state officials visited programs in Colorado, Washington, Texas, and Florida before fashioning their own model. Analysts say the state's racial and ethnic makeup will force designers to be more creative in producing programs that work.

Programs that try to prevent recidivism are cheaper in the long run.

"The whole country is really beginning to move toward the kinds of designs that California is now embracing," says Caren Leaf, director at Lookout Mountain Youth Service Center in Golden, Colo. "States are reframing their objectives with the premise that all these young criminal offenders end up back in local communities. . . . So the overwhelming need is for them to return different than when they left."

Complications to Overcome

California and other states face several hurdles in moving toward a more rehabilitative model. One is funding. California has been struggling to overcome one of its biggest deficits in history. Lawmakers are being pulled in several directions as they look to cut programs from education to welfare.

"The price tag of such reforms is a potential stalling point," says David Steinhart, a California lawyer and juvenile-justice specialist. "If you try to reconfigure and rebuild existing facilities you have to go to the voters and that is a hurdle for the administration."

In the fight over costs, officials are telling lawmakers and citizens alike that programs that try to prevent recidivism are cheaper in the long run. "The concern we have is how much are these offenders going to cost if they come back to the prisons as adults when the cost is even greater," says Leaf.

Another hurdle is the prison culture itself. Many corrections officers worry about going too soft on a prison population that includes some of the state's toughest juvenile offenders. "There is enormous built-in resistance by most of the officers who have been trained, and spent their whole professional life in getting tough on crime," says Carl Mazza, a prison expert at Lehman College, part of the City University of New York. "Many will see that they are being asked to become soft on crime, and many politicians pushing this will be accused of it as well."

Others believe the punishment vs. rehabilitation debate ignores a larger struggle over social values. They say it leaves out discussion of reforming national attitudes about incarceration altogether—and the uneven percentages of blacks, Hispanics, and whites in prison. "Until you have the larger discussion on jobs, civil rights, it's hollow to talk about rehabilitation," says Barry Sanders, a historian at Pitzer College in Claremont, Calif.

9

Juveniles Do Not Understand the Concept of Adult Sentencing

Richard E. Redding

Richard E. Redding is a professor of law at Villanova University School of Law and a research professor of psychology at Drexel University in Pennsylvania. He has published many articles in leading scientific and legal publications.

With the belief that harsh punishment will deter juveniles from committing crimes, most states have imposed "transfer laws," with which violent juvenile offenders are transferred from the juvenile justice system to the adult criminal court system. However, these transfer laws cannot act as a deterrent if juveniles do not understand the laws and believe they will be enforced against them. To determine if they were aware of transfer laws and the possibility of receiving adult sentences, thirty-seven juvenile offenders in DeKalb County, Georgia, were interviewed. Important findings emerged, including that most juveniles were unaware of transfer laws, and the fact that an understanding of the laws may have deterred them from committing the crime in the first place.

An underlying assumption in the nationwide policy shift toward transferring more juveniles to criminal court has been the belief that the threat of stricter, adult sentences will

Richard E. Redding and Elizabeth J. Fuller, "What Do Juvenile Offenders Know About Being Tried as Adults? Implications for Deterrence," *Juvenile and Family Court Journal*, Summer, 2004, pp. 35–37, 39–42. Copyright © 2004 NCJFCJ all rights reserved. Reproduced by permission.

act as either a specific or general deterrent to juvenile crime. But there is little evidence that this goal has been achieved. In terms of specific deterrence, seven recent large-scale studies in various jurisdictions have all found higher recidivism [repeat offending] rates among juveniles tried and sentenced as adults when compared to those tried as juveniles. With respect to general deterrence—i.e., whether transfer laws deter would-be juvenile offenders from committing serious and violent crimes—the picture is considerably less clear, because the few research studies have produced conflicting findings.

Research Is Necessary to Determine Juveniles' Awareness

Clearly, further research is needed to examine whether juvenile transfer laws have general deterrent effects by discouraging and preventing juveniles from committing crime. In particular, it is important to examine whether juveniles are aware of transfer laws, whether this awareness deters delinquent behavior, and whether they believe the laws will be enforced against them. A law cannot act as a deterrent if the targeted population is unaware that the law exists or if the population does not believe it will be enforced, which may partly explain why studies have failed to find general deterrent effects of transfer laws. The threat of criminal punishment may need to reach a minimum threshold of certainty before the threat acts as a deterrent. "A fundamental premise of deterrence theory is that to be effective in preventing crime the threat and application of the law must be made known to the public. . . . [T]he publicity surrounding punishment serves important educative, moralizing, normative validation, and coercive functions." . . .

Although an exploratory study conducted with 37 juvenile offenders in one jurisdiction (the Atlanta, Georgia area), the current study's significance is three-fold. First, following recent expansions in states' transfer laws, it is the first study to examine juveniles' knowledge and perceptions of transfer laws and criminal motions. Second, we interviewed juvenile offenders who had been transferred to criminal court, obtaining quantitative as well as qualitative data based on structured interview questions.

Third, the jurisdiction where the research was conducted is of particular significance. Georgia is one of 31 states that have elected to automatically remove from juvenile court jurisdiction juveniles arrested for certain serious crimes. In 1994, the Georgia legislature passed the School Safety and Juvenile Justice Act, stating:

> The safety of students enrolled in schools and the citizens of Georgia will be enhanced by requiring that certain violent juvenile offenders who commit certain violent felonies be tried as adults in the superior court and sentenced directly to the custody of the Department of Corrections.

The Juvenile Justice System in Georgia

The automatic transfer law provides that juveniles between 13 and 17 who are charged with one of the so-called "seven deadly sins" (murder, voluntary manslaughter, rape, aggravated sexual battery, aggravated sodomy, aggravated child molestation, and armed robbery committed with a firearm) be tried and sentenced as adults in criminal court. Juveniles tried as adults are then subject to Georgia's mandatory minimum sentencing laws, which require 10-year minimum sentences for serious violent felonies. The number of youths affected by the law has been tremendous, and it has disproportionately affected minorities. Between 1994 and 2002, approximately 3,850 juveniles were arrested for one of the "seven deadly sins" in Georgia. Seventy-six percent of all juveniles arrested for these crimes were African-Americans, who represent only 34% of Georgia's juvenile population. The disproportionate representation of African-American youths transferred to the criminal justice system mirrors the overrepresentation of African-Americans in the criminal justice system generally. A recent study by the Georgia State Board of Pardons and Paroles (1999) concluded that "four out of every ten black males (38.5%) will likely go to a Georgia state prison sometime over the course of their lives". In public health terms, this is an epidemic having clear racial disparities.

Importantly, Georgia had undertaken efforts to alert juveniles to its new automatic transfer law by producing a video (called "Multiple Choice") about the law. The video, which also "provides a realistic picture of conditions and life inside Georgia's adult prisons as seen through interviews with incarcerated juveniles," was distributed to schools and prevention programs around the state and was periodically aired on Georgia television. In addition, the Atlanta (DeKalb County) District Attorney's Office distributed an informational brochure about the law to local teens and their parents. Thus, interviewing juveniles in the Atlanta area allowed us to determine their knowledge of the transfer law during a time when some efforts were being made to publicize the consequences of committing serious crimes.

Juvenile Offenders Are Interviewed

Participants included 37 juveniles who had committed armed robbery or armed robbery and felony murder in Georgia. Under Georgia law, they are automatically tried as adults. Thirty-one juveniles were in Atlanta-area (DeKalb County) jails awaiting trial or had been convicted, and six were serving their sentences in state correctional facilities in the Atlanta area.

Ninety-two percent of participants were African-American and 8% were Hispanic or Asian. The percentage of African-Americans in the sample reflects the fact that 91% of all youths arrested in DeKalb County, Georgia, for one of the "seven deadly sins" were African-American. The participants ranged in age from 15 to 20 at the time of the interview (average age = 16.4). The highest grade completed in school ranged from 7th to 11th grade, with the average being 9th grade. The number of prior arrests for these juveniles ranged from 0 to 20, with an average of 4.2 prior arrests. The number of prior juvenile delinquency adjudications [judicial decisions] ranged from 0 to 6, with an average of .94. None of the juveniles had a prior adult criminal conviction.

All juveniles who had been charged as adults in DeKalb County, Georgia, at the time of the study were identified by Atlanta-area public defenders who accompanied researchers to the facilities and introduced the research study to the juveniles. Informed consent was obtained from all participants. Each juvenile was informed that his participation was strictly voluntary, that refusal to participate would not affect his case, and that all responses would be kept anonymous and confidential. Only one juvenile refused to participate.

Participants were individually interviewed for about two hours in a private conference room. The interview protocol, part of a larger study with juvenile offenders, consisted of structured and semi-structured questions asking the juveniles about: (1) their knowledge and understanding of Georgia's transfer law and criminal sanctions for juvenile offenders; (2) perceptions of the law's fairness and whether knowledge of such laws would deter them or other juveniles from committing crimes; (3) how they acquire information about law and punishment; (4) their experiences in adult jails and prisons; and (5) their perceptions of the consequences of criminal behavior. . . .

Many Juveniles Do Not Understand Transfer Laws

Only 30.3% [of study participants] knew before they committed the crime that juveniles could be tried as adults. None thought that they could or would be tried as an adult for the crime they committed. Rather, the juveniles thought they would be tried in juvenile court and receive a sanction of probation, boot camp, or a several-month stay in a juvenile detention facility. As one juvenile said, "When they caught me, I thought my momma would just come get me and I wouldn't even have to spend the night." Repeatedly, the juveniles said "I never knew" or "somebody should have told us" about being tried as adults and the 10-year mandatory minimum sentence.

Most participants felt that trying them as adults was unfair and unjustified because juveniles are immature, careless, "don't take things seriously," or deserve another chance. As one participant asserted, "If you're a juvenile, you should be tried as a juvenile." Thirty-seven percent thought that it never was fair to try juveniles as adults for any crime; only 6.3% felt it fair to try juveniles as adults for armed robbery (the offense for which many were charged). But a few juveniles felt that trying them as adults was justified. One participant said, "I just keep getting slaps on the wrist. . . . I guess they had to do more."

"I thought that since I'm a juvenile I could do just about anything and just get six months if I got caught."

About half of the juveniles understood some of the purposes of transfer laws (e.g., to punish juveniles or to prevent crime), but an equal number did not understand what the law was trying to accomplish by trying them as an adult. One juvenile, for example, thought it was only because his codefendants were being tried as adults. Many of the juveniles were charged with armed robbery, which many did not perceive to be a violent or serious crime. Several participants commented that armed robbery was just a "scare tactic" and did not carry the intent to harm. This perception seemed to contribute to their confusion over receiving a 10-year sentence for that crime. When asked to rank the "seven deadly sins" in order of severity, half the participants ranked murder as the most serious while half ranked rape as the most serious. Many said that rape was the only crime for which it was fair to try juveniles as adults: "Rape really hurts someone and if someone does it, they know what they are doing."

Awareness Would Have Been a Deterrent

Although only 40% of the participants reported considering the chances of getting caught when they committed the offense, they felt the transfer law would have deterred them had they been aware that they could be tried as an adult and receive a lengthy adult sentence. As one juvenile said, "What are you talking about? I'm not doing ten years!" Overall, they felt that the consequences of committing the crime were worse than they had expected. Seventy-six percent thought that being in jail or prison would make it less likely that they would commit crimes in the future; "I don't want to go through this again," one participant commented. In comparison to the sanctions they had received in the juvenile court (which many characterized as "a slap on the wrist"), many felt that their experiences in the criminal justice system had finally taught them that there will be serious consequences if they commit crimes:

> "This ain't no juvenile daycare—I'm facing real time now."

> "[Being tried as an adult] showed me it's not a game anymore. Before, I thought that since I'm a juvenile I could do just about anything and just get six months if I got caught. So, I didn't care and thought I could get away with anything."

The juveniles said they had offended previously in part because they perceived that the chances of getting caught and receiving a serious sanction were slim.

Juveniles whose jail or prison experiences were worse than they had expected were less likely to think it would deter them from committing future crimes. Similarly, juveniles who had experienced beatings while incarcerated and those who knew youths who had been raped while incarcerated, also were less likely to think that their jail or prison experience would deter them from committing crimes in the future.

Finally, participants were asked about effective ways to "get the word out" to other juveniles that they could be tried as adults and receive lengthy sentences for committing serious offenses. The responses were fairly consistent across participants, who suggested public service announcements on radio and television, advertising near nightclubs frequented by teens, and having police officers or judges give talks at boys' clubs, e.g.:

> "After TV wrestling shows would be a good time. Lots of kids watch those. Have another kid doing the ad, like a kid from prison. Then that kid can tell other kids what the deal is. If it is coming from someone who has really been in jail, it will seem real."

> "You leave a nightclub all hyped up. Sometimes when you walk out someone will say, 'Let's go hit this'. . . . If there was a sign right outside the club so that when someone said to go hit a place, you could look up right then and see what the punishment would be. That would make you think twice."

Juveniles Need to Be Made Aware of Transfer Laws

Four key findings emerge from the results. First, juveniles were unaware of the transfer law. Second, they felt that awareness of these laws and the severe penalties may have prevented them from committing the crime or may prevent other juveniles from committing serious crimes, and they suggested practical ways to enhance juveniles' awareness of transfer laws. Third, the juveniles generally felt that it was unfair to try and sentence them as adults. Finally, the consequences of committing their crime were worse than most had imagined, and the harsh consequences of their incarceration in adult facilities may have had a brutalizing effect on some children. Each finding is discussed in turn.

Only a third of the juveniles were aware of the new transfer law, and their knowledge of the law was quite superficial. The video describing the new transfer law was distributed to public schools in Georgia; however, this seemingly was not the most effective strategy for reaching the population at risk. This is not surprising, as the literature is clear that school absence and truancy is very common among serious juvenile offenders. Indeed, in our study, many of the juveniles in the sample were not attending school (they had dropped out, were habitually truant, or had been expelled) when they committed the offense. In addition, showing the video was up to each individual teacher; so even for those few juveniles who were attending school, there was no guarantee that the video would be shown in their classes.

Even among those who knew about the law, none thought it would be enforced against them for the crime they had committed. Indeed, many thought that they would only get "slap on the wrist" sentences from the juvenile court. . . .

Most juveniles felt that knowing they could be tried and sentenced as adults may have prevented them from committing the crime.

However, most juveniles felt that knowing they could be tried and sentenced as adults may have prevented them from committing the crime, that the knowledge would deter them in the future and may prevent other juveniles from committing crimes. We cannot know whether the juveniles' introspections are accurate. However, a recent study with serious juvenile offenders found a correlation between their self-reported likelihood of committing a future offense and the number of offenses they committed after their release, as did a recent study with adult offenders. Some evidence indicates that the certainty of apprehension and punishment is important in deterring adult offenders, and the current study adds to the limited evidence that juvenile offenders may calibrate their behavior as a function of the perceived certainty of punishment. Corrado [Raymond R. Corrado, juvenile justice expert and author], et al.'s (2003) recent study found a negative relationship between intent to reoffend and sentence severity in a sample of serious and violent juvenile offenders. . . .

Policymakers should increase and improve their attempts to make would-be juvenile offenders aware of the consequences of serious and violent crime.

The results suggest the need for better designed and targeted public awareness campaigns on the state and local levels. Policymakers should increase and improve their attempts to make would-be juvenile offenders aware of the consequences of serious and violent crime. Properly targeted public awareness campaigns have proven effective in reducing adult crime in some contexts, and public awareness of a law is a necessary predicate to its acting as a deterrent. There is an urgent need for rigorous public-health research to evaluate the general deterrent impact of community-wide educational campaigns that are intensive and well-targeted toward the population of potential juvenile offenders.

Public health officials can be instrumental in designing, implementing, and evaluating a social marketing campaign to increase awareness of the criminal penalties for serious crime vis-à-vis the juvenile populations most at risk. Social marketing, a technique that combines the tools of public health marketing and behavior change theory, recognizes that careful attention must be paid to the nature of the behavior to be promoted or avoided, the ways in which the message will be delivered, and the costs people perceive they will have to pay to begin or discontinue behavior. Social marketing has proven effective in other public health epidemics in reducing risky behavior and promoting behavior change. Examples can be found in reductions in teenage smoking and drunk-driving rates following such campaigns. An important facet of social marketing is to elicit the help of the target population in developing the message, identifying proper messengers, and pinpointing the appropriate means of distribution of the health message. The juveniles in our study provided important tips on how most effectively to increase awareness among their peers. They suggested public service announcements on TV and radio, advertising near nightclubs, and having police or judges give talks at boys' clubs. Further conversations and the development of a social marketing plan are warranted.

10

Adolescents Are Not Competent to Stand Trial

MacArthur Foundation Research Network on Adolescent Development and Juvenile Justice

The Research Network on Adolescent Development and Juvenile Justice is an interdisciplinary, multi-institutional program focused on building a foundation of sound science and legal scholarship to support reform of the juvenile justice system.

The American justice system demands that those who are accused of committing a crime must be mentally competent to understand and participate in their trials. Because of the increasing number of juveniles coming to trial, the MacArthur Foundation Research Network on Adolescent Development and Juvenile Justice performed a study to determine if the inherent emotional and psychological immaturity of adolescents deems them incompetent to participate in their own defense. The study found that youth under the age of fifteen are significantly impaired in their ability to understand criminal proceedings and comprehend the risks of their decisions. As an example, younger teens are willing to confess to a crime if they think they will be allowed to go home. The findings from this study reveal that youth need special protection from court proceedings because of their immaturity and, thus, incompetence to stand trial.

One of the pillars of the American justice system is the assurance that those who stand accused of crimes be mentally competent to understand and participate in their trials.

MacArthur Foundation Research Network on Adolescent Development and Juvenile Justice, "Issue Brief #1: Adolescent Legal Competence in Court," *MacArthur Foundation Research Network on Adolescent Development and Juvenile Justice*, September, 2006. Reproduced by permission.

The conventional standard for competence has typically focused on the effects of mental illness or mental retardation on individuals' capacities to grasp the nature of their trials or their abilities to decide how to plead. Yet as the courts, both juvenile and adult, see increasingly younger defendants some argue that the law should also take into account adolescents' lesser capacities owing to emotional and psychological immaturity.

This brief details findings from the first comprehensive assessment of juvenile capacities to participate in criminal proceedings using measures of both trial-related abilities and developmental maturity. The MacArthur Foundation Research Network on Adolescent Development and Juvenile Justice compared the responses of youth and adults in a series of hypothetical legal situations, such as plea bargains, police interrogations, and attorney-client interactions. Responses revealed the degree to which participants understood the long-term consequences of their decisions, their ability to weigh risks, and other factors related to developmental and cognitive maturity. Findings show that a significant portion of youth, especially under age 15, are likely unable to participate competently in their own trials, either in an adult or juvenile court, owing to developmental immaturity.

It is important to note that our study examined only youths' competence to stand trial, not their criminal blameworthiness (i.e., whether someone should be held fully responsible for an offense). These are two separate issues. For example, a young inexperienced driver who accidentally skidded off the road and killed another person might be competent to stand trial for the wrongful death of another, but could be judged less than fully responsible for the death because it was accidental. Whether youths of a certain age have abilities suggesting competence or incompetence to stand trial does not tell us whether youths of that age should or should not be held as responsible as adults for their offenses.

Young Adolescents Are Likely to Lack Capacities for Trial

Network researchers interviewed 1,400 individuals aged 11–24 both in juvenile detention centers and in the community at large to determine whether teens differed from young adults (aged 18–24) in their abilities relevant for competence to stand trial. Youth were interviewed in Philadelphia, Los Angeles, northern Florida, and Virginia.

Using a standard assessment tool, the study first gauged the functional abilities defined in the existing legal concept of *competence to proceed*—the ability to understand the purpose and nature of the trial process; the capacity to provide relevant information to counsel and to process that information; and the ability to apply information to one's own situation in a manner that is neither distorted nor irrational. This standard is regularly applied in adult courts with mentally impaired individuals.

Findings from the assessment showed that age matters. Those aged 11–13 performed significantly worse than 14–15 year olds, who performed significantly worse than 16–17 year olds and 18–24 year olds (adults). Interestingly, the performance of 16–17 year olds did not differ from that of the young adults (aged 18–24).

The youngest group was nearly three times more likely than youth older than 15 to be significantly impaired in reasoning and understanding, two important components of legal competence. In other words, nearly one-third of 11–13 year olds and one-fifth of 14–15 year olds had deficits that courts might see as serious enough to question their ability to proceed in a trial. These patterns varied little by race-ethnicity, gender, socioeconomic status, or region of the country.

Level of Maturity Influences Important Choices

The Network next assessed youths' emotional maturity in a legal decision-making context. The most relevant aspects of maturity in this context are the ability to take into consideration long-term consequences (future orientation), perceive and comprehend risks, deflect peer influence, and weigh whether to comply with authority figures.

> *Younger individuals were more likely to endorse decisions that comply with what an authority [figure] seemed to want.*

Using the *MacArthur Judgment Evaluation*, a tool designed specifically for this study, researchers asked respondents to recommend the best and worst choices in three hypothetical situations: responding to police interrogation when one is guilty of a crime; disclosing information during consultation with a defense attorney; and responding to a plea agreement in exchange for a guilty plea and testimony against other defendants. Choices for police interrogation included confessing, denying the offense, or refusing to speak. Choices for the attorney consultation included full or partial disclosure, denial, or refusing to cooperate. Plea agreement options included accepting or rejecting the offer. Researchers also asked participants to identify the positive and negative consequences (or risks) of each of their recommendations, and their responses were scored according to predetermined criteria for risk appraisal. Researchers measured youths' future orientation from these responses. Finally, to assess the influence of peer pressure, youth were told to imagine that their friends had chosen a different response and were given the option of changing their answer.

> *Younger teens were significantly less likely to recognize the inherent risks in various decisions.*

In general, the youngest teens (aged 11–13) proved less mature in their decision making than older youth. Younger individuals, for example, were more likely to endorse decisions that comply with what an authority [figure] seemed to want as measured by their willingness to confess and plea bargain. The proportion of youth who recommended confession decreased with age, from about one-half of the 11–13 year olds to only one-fifth of the 18–24 year olds. (Few individuals in any age group chose to actively deny the offense.) The proportion who advised accepting a plea agreement declined from nearly three-fourths of 11–13 year olds to one-half of young adults. Once again, the study revealed few statistically significant differences among those older than age 15.

In addition, younger teens were significantly less likely to recognize the inherent risks in various decisions, and they were less likely to comprehend the long-term consequences of their decisions. The study found no differences by age in the effects of peer pressure on decision making. Those with lower IQs, however, performed more poorly on all items. Although perhaps not surprising, this finding is notable given that two-thirds of those under age 15 in juvenile detention facilities had an IQ lower than 89 compared with one-third in the community sample. Therefore, because a greater proportion of youth in the juvenile justice system are of below-average intelligence, the risk for incompetence to stand trial is even greater among adolescents who are in the juvenile justice system than it is among adolescents in the community. For example, among 11–13 year olds with very low IQ scores, more than one-half scored as poorly as adults who are typically found incompetent to stand trial. Once again, none of the findings varied by race-ethnicity, socioeconomic status, or locale.

These findings suggest that younger adolescents' developmental immaturity may affect their behavior as defendants in ways that extend beyond their competence to stand trial. Their responses indicate that they are often more willing than adults to confess to authority figures such as police, rather than remaining silent, especially if they believe it will result in an immediate reward, such as going home. For similar reasons, they may be more willing to accept a prosecutor's plea agreement.

Expanded Definition of Competence Needed

Clearly, many of the youngest adolescents are less able to understand the trial process and are less mature in their ability to take into consideration the long-term ramifications of their decisions. Yet, the relation between immaturity and competence to stand trial has not yet been defined legally. The findings reported here point to the need for a broader legal construct of competency, one that recognizes that developmental factors–namely, cognitive and psychosocial immaturity—may compromise the critical decision-making ability of many young criminal defendants in either adult or juvenile courts. The findings also suggest the need to consider various protections against trying youth who may not be competent; for example, making competency evaluations mandatory for adolescents below a certain age, and requiring competence evaluations for any youth sent to criminal court to be tried as an adult.

The findings raise a dilemma, however. If a sizable proportion of younger adolescents are unfit to stand trial owing to immaturity, how does society redress the crimes they committed? One option is to develop a dual system of competence, one for the adult courts and one for the juvenile courts, with more relaxed standards of competence in the latter. Youth deemed incompetent to stand trial in an adult court could be tried in a juvenile court under less demanding standards of competence. Of course, this lower standard of protection would also require less punitive sentencing that involves rehabilitative services for those youth. For those very few who would be deemed incompetent to stand trial in either court, dismissal of charges and adequate supervision with useful remedial services could be employed, as is already done in many states.

New Guides to Help Assess Juvenile Competence

Legal and clinical practitioners have had few, if any, resources to help them understand how immaturity manifests itself in legal contexts with juveniles. . . .

The findings of this latest research affirm the developmental reality of adolescence and underscore the need to expand the notion of competence to include cognitive and psychosocial maturity. The competency standard announced by the Supreme Court in *Dusky v. United States* (1960) is a functional test, and functionally it should make no difference whether the source of the defendant's incompetence is mental illness (the current standard for adults) or immaturity.

11

Minors Are Not as Blameworthy as Adults

Human Rights Watch

Human Rights Watch, an independent, nongovernmental organization, is dedicated to protecting the human rights of people around the world.

Because children have not fully matured, either physically or mentally, they should not be held to the same standards of accountability as adults. Psychological research has shown that adolescents have not yet developed the capability to fully consider long-term consequences, which causes them to react impulsively and emotionally rather than rationally. Anatomically speaking, magnetic resonance imaging (MRI) tests reveal that the frontal lobes in a teenager's brain have not developed sufficiently to regulate aggression or to understand the consequences of a particular action. For these reasons, minors should not be considered as blameworthy as adults, and justice would be better served if child offenders were sentenced with rehabilitative principles in mind.

It is axiomatic [self-evident] that children are in the process of growing up, both physically and mentally. Their forming identities make young offenders excellent candidates for rehabilitation—they are far more able than adults to learn new skills, find new values, and re-embark on a better, law-abiding life. Justice is best served when these rehabilitative principles,

Human Rights Watch, "The Rest of Their Lives: Life Without Parole for Child Offenders in the United States, Chapter V: The Difference Between Youth and Adults," New York, NY: Human Rights Watch, 2005. Copyright © 2005 Human Rights Watch. Reproduced by permission.

at the core of human rights standards, are at the heart of any punishments imposed on child offenders. Sentences must take into account both the gravity of the crime as well as the culpability or blameworthiness of the offender. The question of culpability is what separates children from adults. While children can commit acts as violent and deadly as those adults commit, their blameworthiness is different by virtue of their immaturity. Their punishment should acknowledge that substantial difference.

Children may know right from wrong: proponents of adult sentences for children correctly point out that most children, even a six-year-old, can parrot the phrase that it is "wrong" to kill, albeit often without any real understanding of what killing means or why it is wrong. But by virtue of their immaturity, children have less developed capacities than adults to control their impulses, to use reason to guide their behavior, and to think about the consequences of their conduct. They are, in short, still "growing up." A sentence of life without parole negates that reality, treating child offenders as though their characters are already irrevocably set.

The Difference According to Psychology

Psychological research confirms what every parent knows: children, including teenagers, act more irrationally and immaturely than adults. According to many psychologists, adolescents are less able than adults to perceive and understand the long-term consequences of their acts, to think autonomously instead of bending to peer pressure or the influence of older friends and acquaintances, and to control their emotions and act rationally instead of impulsively. All of these tendencies affect a child's ability to make reasoned decisions.

Psychologists have long attributed the differences between adults and children to either cognitive or psychosocial differences. Cognitive theories suggest that children simply think differently than adults, while psychosocial explanations propose that children lack social and emotional capabilities that are better developed in adults.

Even mature young people will often revert to more child-like and impulsive decision-making processes under extreme pressure.

Research has established that adolescent thinking is present-oriented and tends to either ignore or discount future outcomes and implications. At least one researcher has found that teenagers typically have a very short time-horizon, looking only a few days into the future when making decisions. Another study concluded that only 25 percent of tenth graders (whose average age is sixteen), compared to 42 percent of twelfth graders (whose average age is eighteen), considered the long-term consequences of important decisions. To the extent that adolescents do consider the implications of their acts, they emphasize short-term consequences, perceiving and weighing longer-term consequences to a lesser degree.

Psychological research also consistently demonstrates that children have a greater tendency than adults to make decisions based on emotions, such as anger or fear, rather than logic and reason. Studies further confirm that stressful situations only heighten the risk that emotion, rather than rational thought, will guide the choices children make.

In the most emotionally taxing circumstances, children are less able to use whatever high-level reasoning skills they may possess, meaning that even mature young people will often revert to more child-like and impulsive decision-making processes under extreme pressure.

Gregory C., who was fifteen when he shot and killed a police officer who had pulled him over for speeding in a stolen car, described his state of mind at the time:

A kid just does something—whether it's an accident or intentional. I mean personally, me, I was fifteen years old. . . . I didn't know what I was doing. I was still a kid. . . . Kids do a lot of stupid things. . . . The person I was when I was fifteen, I really didn't have any morals, I didn't even know who I was at that time. I hate to admit it, but I was real ignorant.

The Difference According to Neuroscience

Neuroscientists using magnetic resonance imaging (MRI) to study the brain are now providing a physiological explanation for the features of adolescence that developmental psychologists—as well as parents and teachers—have identified for years. These MRI studies reveal that children have physiologically less-developed means of controlling themselves.

Neuroscientists have produced MRI images of the anatomy and function of the brain at different ages and while an individual performs a range of tasks. They have uncovered striking differences between the brains of adolescents and those of adults. Much of this scientific research into the biological distinctions between adults and children reveals that these differences occur along an age continuum—they do not magically disappear at a given age—and the rate at which the adolescent brain acquires adult capabilities differs from individual to individual. Nevertheless, researchers have identified broad patterns of change in adolescents that begin with puberty and continue into young adulthood.

A key difference between adolescent and adult brains concerns the frontal lobe. The frontal lobe of teenagers is composed of different quantities and types of cell matter and has different neural features than the adult brain. Researchers have linked the frontal lobe (especially a part of the frontal lobe called the prefrontal cortex) to "regulating aggression, long-range planning, mental flexibility, abstract thinking, the capacity to hold in mind related pieces of information, and perhaps moral judgment." In children, the frontal lobe has not developed sufficiently to perform these functions. Throughout puberty, the frontal lobe undergoes substantial transformations that increase the individual's ability to undertake decision-making that projects into future and to weigh rationally the consequences of a particular course of action.

These cells and neural developments in the brain provide an anatomical basis for concluding that youth up to age eighteen are, on average, less responsible for criminal acts than adults.

These cell and neural developments in the brain provide an anatomical basis for concluding that youth up to age eighteen are, on average, less responsible for criminal acts than adults. As Daniel Weinberger, director of the Clinical Brain Disorders Laboratory at the National Institutes of Health, explains, the developed frontal lobe, including its prefrontal cortex, "allows us to act on the basis of reason. It can preclude an overwhelming tendency for action. . . . It also allows us to consciously control our tendency to have impulsive behavior."

Addressing youth violence, Weinberger explains:

> I doubt that most school shooters intended to kill, in the adult sense of permanently ending a life and paying the consequences for the rest of their lives. Such intention would require a mature prefrontal cortex, which could anticipate the future and rationally appreciate cause and effect. . . . The [juvenile] brain does not have the biological machinery to inhibit impulses in the service of long-term planning.

In addition, because their frontal lobe functions poorly, adolescents tend to use a part of the brain called the amygdala during their decision-making. The amygdala is a locus for impulsive and aggressive behavior, and its dominance over the undeveloped frontal lobe makes adolescents "more prone to react with gut instincts." In adult brains, the frontal lobe offers a check on the emotions and impulses originating from the amygdala. Reflecting on the dominance of the amygdala, Deborah Yurgelun-Todd of the Harvard Medical School concluded:

> [A]dolescents are more prone to react with gut instinct when they process emotions but as they mature into early adulthood, they are able to temper their instinctive gut reaction response with rational, reasoned responses. . . . Adult brains use the frontal lobe to rationalize or apply brakes to emotional responses. Adolescent brains are just beginning to develop that ability.

12

Minority Youth Are Disproportionately Imprisoned

Ellis Cose

Ellis Cose, a columnist and contributing editor for Newsweek, *is the author of many books, including* Bone to Pick: On Forgiveness, Reconciliation, Reparation and Revenge *and* The Envy of the World: On Being a Black Man in America.

Most Americans assume that the more people are put in jail, the greater the public safety. They also believe that racism is not a factor in the justice system. Both assumptions are incorrect. It is becoming increasingly clear that locking up young people turns them into career criminals. And of those young people who are detained in public facilities, two-thirds are persons of color. A study in Washington State reveals significant racial stereotyping in juvenile cases, and another study by a team from a Chicago investigative magazine shows that blacks and Latinos generally receive harsher sentences than whites who commit the same crimes. A change in policy is clearly needed. Instead of committing juvenile offenders to adult facilities, early intervention and rehabilitative programs will have a greater impact on reducing crime, and ultimately will even out racially disparate treatment.

As an attorney for the Youth Law Center, litigating largely over conditions of confinement, James Bell spent some 20 years in courtrooms across America. The scene was always much the same: Even in communities that were overwhelm-

Ellis Cose, "Race and Redemption," *The American Prospect*, August 14, 2005. Copyright © 2005 The American Prospect, Inc. All rights reserved. Reproduced with permission from *The American Prospect*, 11 Beacon Street, Suite 1120, Boston, MA 02108.

ingly white, those arrested, detained, and convicted were over-whelmingly black and brown. Nonwhites, as Bell saw it, were being "Velcroed in" as whites were "Tefloned out."

The statistics are now so well-known they have almost lost their ability to shock: roughly 2 million men behind bars, the majority of whom are Latino and black. At every juncture—from suspicion to conviction—people of color, especially blacks, are significantly more likely than whites to get tangled up in America's system of justice. And juvenile statistics mirror those for adults: Roughly two-thirds of juveniles detained in public facilities are persons of color—nearly twice their proportion in the general population. If you are young, Latino, and male, your odds of being in juvenile detention are more than twice those of your Anglo counterpart. If you are Native American, odds are three times as likely. If you are black, five times as likely. We have reached the point where the only bond linking many black fathers, sons, and grandsons is time spent behind bars. Imagine a great conveyer belt onto which will stumble a third of America's black males (if current trends continue), leading toward confinement and away from every positive option in life, and you have some sense of the crises upon us.

People sitting in judgment often "have no idea about the lives of the people they are imposing conditions on."

Seeking to Reverse the Trend

Bell's front-row seat at the justice factory impelled him to try to turn those statistics around. Nearly four years ago [2001], he launched the W. Haywood Burns Institute for Juvenile Justice Fairness and Equity. Based in San Francisco and named for a crusading black attorney, the institute aspires to snatch young people off the conveyor belt before their nobler aspirations are irremediably crushed. And it is already having an impact.

In the communities in which it works, the institute tries to bring together all so-called stakeholders—judges, police, public defenders, community organizations, probation-department officials, and others who don't ordinarily collaborate. One purpose is simple education: People sitting in judgment often "have no idea about the lives of the people they are imposing conditions on," observed Bell. But the larger purpose is to find a common plan of action. That may mean seeking alternatives to confinement for nonviolent parole violators. In Chicago and Sacramento, California, the process has led to the creation of evening reporting centers. Young offenders are picked up after school and taken to a gathering place, where they are fed, helped with their homework, and taught something about different options in life.

In a field defined almost exclusively by very bad news, the good news is that Bell is not alone. Even as an alarmist mass media and slogan-chanting politicians have focused on "super-predators" wreaking havoc on society, more reasoned minds have come to agree with the commonsensical view that "14-year-olds are almost never beyond any form of redemption," in the words of Christina Swarns, director of the criminal-justice program of the NAACP [National Association for the Advancement of Colored People] Legal Defense and Educational Fund.

Blacks and Latinos generally got stiffer penalties than whites who had committed the same drug crimes.

The Annie E. Casey Foundation's Juvenile Detention Alternatives Initiative (JDAI), launched in 1992, was inspired in large measure by a Casey Foundation–funded project in Broward County, Florida, aimed at reducing the number of young people behind bars. According to the foundation's Bart Lubow, the initiative runs "against the grain of a fundamental mythology" that more people behind bars automatically leads to greater public safety. It also runs contrary to the widespread assumption that race and racism have essentially been banished from the justice system.

Racism in the Justice System

That assumption is not yet supported by facts. In a review of 233 juvenile cases in Washington state, sociologists George Bridges and Sara Steen found that racial stereotyping played an unmistakable role in how offenders were viewed. Probation officers preparing sentencing reports tended to characterize whites as potentially good people who were victims of unfortunate circumstances, whereas blacks were more likely to be seen as intrinsically bad, according to their study published in the *American Sociological Review* in 1998. Not coincidentally, after analyzing six years of court records, a team from *The Chicago Reporter* found in 2002 that blacks and Latinos generally got stiffer penalties than whites who had committed the same drug crimes.

For its pilot program, the foundation identified five JDAI sites: Cook County, Illinois; Milwaukee County, Wisconsin; Multnomah County, Oregon; New York City; and Sacramento County, California. By 1998, only three sites remained. The powers that be in both New York (by this time Rudolph Giuliani had become mayor) and Milwaukee had lost their enthusiasm for any programs that could be perceived as soft on perpetrators. Cook, Multnomah, and Sacramento counties pressed ahead. Santa Cruz, California, and King County, Washington, joined along the way. The approach the JDAI pioneered is essentially that now employed by Bell's W. Haywood Burns Institute.

In Cook County (Chicago), all participants realized that the vast majority of youths detained were people of color, mostly blacks, but there was no real consensus about what role race played in the process. As a result, the Chicago initiative focused much less on race than on reducing the numbers of youths in detention overall. Between 1996 and 2000, the number dropped 31 percent—although people of color continued to constitute the vast majority of those detained.

In Multnomah County (Portland), the results were even more dramatic. Between 1994 and 2000, the number of youths detained dropped by more than 50 percent, and statistics that had previously shown racially disparate treatment began to even out.

Caring About Minority Kids

There is no "silver programmatic bullet," Lubow observes. Creating a saner, more equitable juvenile-justice system requires specific local actions tailored to local conditions, on a range of fronts from staffing to policing to nurturing relationships among stakeholders. The Casey Foundation also found that without explicitly focusing on racial disparity, localities were not likely to do much to reduce it—notwithstanding the fact that all racial disparities do not stem from explicit bias. In Illinois, for instance, a law that required that juveniles be tried as adults if caught selling drugs within 1,000 feet of a school ended up affecting mostly nonwhites—because white drug dealers, operating in the more spatially dispersed suburbs, were less likely to be near schools.

We somehow care much less about urban violence, especially when it involves minority kids.

The number of JDAI sites has now grown to 50. Increasingly, knowledgeable people are appreciating that there are "a whole bunch of deleterious impacts to locking up kids in detention center[s]," in the words of Jason Ziedenberg, executive director of the Justice Policy Institute. Some of the worst impacts are obviously on the young people themselves, who, among other things, are likely to have a radically shortened lifespan due to violence. Researchers at Northwestern University found that juveniles in Cook County who had been in detention were more than four times as likely to die (over an eight-year period) than their matched peers who had managed to avoid being locked up. Of the 65 deaths that researchers recorded during the study, all were violent. "Everyone died awful, violent deaths—run over by gang members, stabbed by a boyfriend," Linda Teplin, a member of the Northwestern team, told a reporter for *HealthDay News.* Teplin went on to observe that the number of deaths among the youngsters she studied in Cook County was higher than the total death toll in all mass school shootings between 1990 and 2000. Yet while concern was showered on those largely white victims of mass murder, little was shown for the mostly minority victims of Cook County. "We somehow care much less about urban violence, especially when it involves minority kids," Teplin concluded.

Whether or not politicians care less about such kids, more and more are realizing that locking up young people and figuratively throwing away the key is an expensive policy failure. As a growing body of research is coming to show, early and sensible intervention reduces the likelihood that young offenders will end up as adult criminals. Young wrongdoers are less likely to err again if they are kept out of adult facilities, where they generally become not only more accepting of a life of crime but also more comfortable with committing more serious crimes.

Despite what used to be received wisdom—"nothing works"—it is becoming very clear that some things do work, that it is possible to simultaneously reduce the burden of young offenders on society, increase their odds of success in life, and eliminate much of the bias in the system. That does not necessarily mean that the old ways are dead. It does mean, however, that they should be. For, tough-on-crime rhetoric notwithstanding, it is becoming harder than ever to justify putting young people on that giant conveyer belt that by-passes hope and heads directly to hell.

13

Experts Disagree Whether Juveniles Should Appear in Court Shackled

Martha T. Moore

Martha T. Moore, a graduate of Yale University, is a writer for USA Today.

Many states require that juvenile offenders be shackled when they appear before a judge in juvenile court. Attorneys who represent juvenile defendants are increasingly challenging this rule, however, claiming that shackling is shameful, disrespectful, terrifying, and can negatively influence judges. More and more judges are agreeing with the attorneys, too, and suggesting that juveniles be handcuffed only on a case-by-case basis. On the other hand, some juvenile justice officials believe that shackling is necessary for security reasons because teenagers often act impulsively and may attempt to escape. Also, when several youths are brought into a courtroom together, shackles prevent them from ganging up on court officers. The debate comes down to what is more important—the rights of juvenile defendants or the safety of the public.

Handcuffs pin the teenage girl's wrists together. The cuffs connect to a heavy chain around her waist so she can't raise her arms. Another chain connects her ankles, shortening her step as she shuffles into the courtroom. When she shifts in her chair, the shackles clink.

Martha T. Moore, "Should Juveniles Go to Court in Chains?" *www.USATODAY.com*, June 17, 2007. Copyright © 2007, *USA Today*. Reproduced by permission.

Malyra Perez is 14, and yes, her mother says, she is trouble-some. Malyra runs away and goes to school high, her mother tells the judge. She is in court on a charge of grand theft auto.

But she shouldn't be in shackles, Myra Perez says. "I didn't like that, not at all. She's not a criminal."

Such sentiments are being heard in courts across the nation, where there are increasingly vigorous debates over rules that require metal shackles to be used on youths who appear at juvenile court hearings.

At issue is whether kids as young as 10 need to be shackled for court security, and whether putting chains on young defendants not only makes them look like criminals but also makes them more likely to think of themselves in that way.

The U.S. Supreme Court has said repeatedly that the sight of shackles on a defendant in a courtroom can unfairly influence a jury. Adult defendants may appear in court in shackles, but not in front of a jury that decides their fate.

In almost all juvenile proceedings, though, a defendant's fate is in the hands of a judge, not a jury. Juvenile court procedures vary among the states and even within counties, so it's unclear precisely how many juvenile courts routinely shackle young defendants. But *USA TODAY* has found that in 28 states, some juvenile courts routinely keep defendants in restraints during court appearances.

Judges increasingly believe shackling children is wrong.

Routine shackling is a better-safe-than-sorry approach, many juvenile justice officials say. Teenage impulsiveness can lead to an escape attempt or an attack on a lawyer, judge or spectator, they say, and outdated security in some courtrooms and inadequate manpower heighten the risk.

Twice a day here in Palm Beach County [Florida], groups of teenagers who have been arrested shuffle into the courtroom, their ankles and wrists shackled, for their initial appearance before a judge. When their cases are called, they sit shackled at the defense table with their court-appointed attorneys.

Whether the judge sends them back to detention or releases them, they leave the courtroom the same way, even those small enough to walk under the arm of the sheriff's deputy holding the door.

Judges Differ on Practice

In state after state, such scenes have inspired attorneys who represent children to launch efforts to have the chains removed. A series of court decisions has shown that judges increasingly believe shackling children is wrong:

- In Florida, judges in Miami-Dade County ruled in December [2006] against routine shackling after a motion by the public defender's office pointed out that juveniles were shackled and adult defendants in similar situations were not.

Shackling is "a shameful practice that is rooted in the horrible racist past of this country."

"You go to a juvenile courtroom and you see a child shackled like a wild animal, and you go over to the adult courtroom and the adult is not shackled," says Carlos Martinez, assistant chief public defender.

Chaining black or Hispanic juvenile defendants carries racial overtones that make the experience worse for the kids involved, he says. Shackling is "a shameful practice that is rooted in the horrible racist past of this country."

A similar motion in nearby Broward County also succeeded. But in Palm Beach County, juvenile judges refused to end shackling, saying in their ruling that the lawyers challenging the practice had not proved that it harmed children and had not evaluated how lifting the rule would affect security. The case is now before an appeals court.

"The whole experience of juvenile court can have a meaningful impact on children, on their respect for the law and their respect for the court system, that can translate into how they behave when they grow up," Palm Beach public defender Carey Haughwout says. "They give respect when they're given respect, and shackling is treating them very disrespectfully."

- In North Carolina, Legal Aid lawyers for a 14-year-old girl in Greensboro asked a judge in February [2007] to remove shackles for court appearances. The lawyers said shackling traumatized the girl, who as a younger child had been sexually abused while handcuffed. In court, the girl was in leg irons and handcuffs attached to a waist chain.

"She was crying," says Ann-Marie Dooley, one of the lawyers who filed the motion. "She could barely lift her hands to wipe her tears." The girl's case is pending.

In March [2007], Guilford County Chief District Court Judge Joseph Turner decided not to end routine shackling there after another teenager in chains, a 16-year-old boy, tried to escape custody while being driven to the courthouse.

- In Connecticut, juvenile courts stopped shackling youths in March [2007], except when judges decide that certain children require restraints. Now, about 30% of kids in court are in some kind of cuffs, based on assessments made by juvenile detention staff and approved by a judge, says Judge Barbara Quinn, deputy chief court administrator. "It's being implemented in the way we intended, because we figured a fair number of young people have a history of violence," Quinn says.

- In California, an appeals court ruled in May [2007] that shackles could be used on minors in a Los Angeles County juvenile court only on a case-by-case basis.

- In North Dakota, the state Supreme Court ruled in March [2007] that a court violated the rights of a 17-year-old boy by not determining whether his request to have his handcuffs removed during trial could be granted. At least two other state supreme courts have ruled against shackling juveniles in court: Illinois in 1977 and Oregon in 1995.

Shackles Create a Negative Perception

Advocates for juveniles say policies that require all young defendants to be shackled are unnecessary because most kids who appear in juvenile courts are there for non-violent offenses. Instead, the advocates say, children should be shackled only if a judge agrees they are likely to be violent or to try to escape.

In 2002, the latest year for which figures are available, less than one-quarter of juvenile delinquency cases that reached court involved assault or more violent crimes, according to the Justice Department. Almost 40% of the 1.6 million cases were for property crimes. There are no national figures for violent incidents in juvenile courtrooms.

The sight of a youth in handcuffs and leg irons could influence the judge's assessment of a child.

Shackling "is so egregious, so offensive, so unnecessary," says Patricia Puritz, executive director of the National Juvenile Defender Center, a group for lawyers who represent children in juvenile courts. "There is harm to the child and there is also harm to the integrity of the process. These children haven't even been found guilty of anything."

Martinez says that "in most of the cases in juvenile court, most of the kids plead guilty. They're pleading guilty while they're in shackles. If that's not a coerced plea, I don't know what is."

No one has studied whether young defendants who are chained in court fare worse than those who are not. Juvenile advocates fear that the sight of a youth in handcuffs and leg irons could influence the judge's assessment of a child and the case at hand.

- "It has the same effect that a judge wearing a robe has," says Bill Briggs, a court-appointed lawyer in rural Modoc County, Calif., where juveniles are shackled during court appearances. "It creates . . . a negative perception."

- "You look guilty," says Abby Anderson of the Connecticut Juvenile Justice Alliance. "You look violent and dangerous, and most kids who come into juvenile court are scared out of their minds and just did something stupid."

Shackling Is Done for Security

In jurisdictions where shackles are used on adults and children in courts, the practice is contrary to the rationale of having a separate court for young people, some critics say.

"The purpose of children's court is to rehabilitate, protect and take care of children," says Rory Rank, a public defender in Las Cruces, N.M., who is petitioning the county juvenile court to end shackling. "If they're treated with dignity in that courtroom, I think it has a lasting effect on them."

Those who believe shackling is necessary to ensure safety say young defendants have less self-control than adults. "They're more inclined to run than adults. They act completely on impulse. They're not getting, sometimes, the gravity of the situation," says Greg Conrad, president of the Court Officers' and Deputies' Association. Although handcuffing teenagers "appears tough, people with experience in the field would actually say it saves everybody a lot of trouble."

In Jacksonville [Florida], where adult and juvenile defendants are shackled—except in front of a jury for adults—small courtrooms with inadequate separation between spectators and defendants make restraints necessary, state's attorney Harry Shorstein says. He gained a national reputation for reducing juvenile crime in the 1990s by prosecuting more juveniles as adults.

Taking handcuffs and leg irons off defendants would require more security personnel, Shorstein says. When as many as a dozen youths are brought into a courtroom together and must wait their turn to go before the judge, he says, shackles keep them from ganging up on court officers. "It's not really a philosophical or criminal justice issue; it's really a lack-of-facilities issue," he says.

In West Palm Beach, Vickie Cramer's son Alan was the first of nine juveniles who went before Judge Moses Baker Jr. on the same afternoon as Malyra Perez. The 16-year-old was charged with criminal mischief, grand theft auto and aggravated battery with a deadly weapon after he smashed his mother's door and windows with a baseball bat and drove away in his father's car.

"It's shocking to see him like that. It's sad to see him like that," Cramer says of the handcuffs and leg irons her son wore. Then she adds, "Actually, I think it's a good thing. He needs to know the severity of what's going on."

The outcome of juvenile cases is confidential, but Cramer says Alan later pleaded guilty to lesser charges of criminal mischief and possession of a firearm. Her account could not be verified independently because the court records are sealed. Alan will be under house arrest with an electronic ankle bracelet until he is assigned by the judge in July [2007], to a juvenile facility, she says.

In West Virginia, juvenile courtrooms are closed to the public. Even so, Denny Dodson, deputy director of the Division of Juvenile Services, believes that young defendants find appearing in shackles so embarrassing that it may motivate them to stay out of trouble in the future.

"In some ways, it's embarrassing to the point of they don't want it to happen again," he says. "To have to wear shackles in front of your mom or your grandmother may well be more positive than negative. They just don't want that to happen. They hate that."

A Matter of Respect

Judge Dale Koch has seen children in his court with shackles and without. For years, juvenile defendants in his Portland, Ore., courtroom wore them. He says that didn't affect his impression of the defendants, whose backgrounds he already knew.

But being shackled meant youths had trouble handling paperwork and writing with their hands in cuffs, says Koch, president of the National Council of Juvenile and Family Court Judges. And it could have motivated them to agree to plea bargains simply to get out of shackles, he says. "Unfortunately, that is how their reasoning process works," Koch says.

In 1995, an Oregon appeals court sent back a case he had presided over, ruling he should have determined whether there was a reason to shackle the defendant before allowing it. Since then, youths appearing in Multnomah County juvenile courts have been unchained. Koch has come to believe it's better that way.

"My experience has been that it can be done safely, as long as you have an exception built in where you can decide that under circumstances of that youth, they need to be shackled," Koch says. "It is just more respectful to not have the kids shackled while they're . . . in front of the judge."

Handcuffs and leg irons are not intended to punish young defendants but are used to protect others in the courtroom from potential violence, says Hunter Hurst, director of the National Center for Juvenile Justice, a Justice Department–funded research organization.

Wearing chains does, however, change a person's appearance, Hurst says. "Of course, you and I both look like someone else in shackles. We don't look better, we look worse. Therein lies, I guess, one of the conundrums that often face justice: What do you do? Do you risk the audience or do you vilify the person on trial?"

14

The Juvenile Justice System Should Be Reformed

Barry Krisberg

Barry Krisberg is president of the National Council on Crime and Delinquency, which is based in Oakland, California.

From the early 1970s through the 1980s, the juvenile justice system in many states moved away from abusive youth prisons and turned instead to community-based programs that emphasized education and rehabilitation. The result was a reduction in the frequency and severity of juvenile crime. But for some unexplained reason—possibly teen drug addiction or high unemployment—the rate of serious violent juvenile crime rose by more than one-third in the early 1990s, causing the American public to panic. Congressional leaders demanded tougher treatment of youth offenders, and the juvenile justice system reverted back to punishment and incarceration. However, in 1993 research by the Justice Department's Comprehensive Strategy for Serious, Violent, and Chronic Juvenile Offenders showed that only a small number of offenders committed the most serious crimes. Other juvenile-justice officials advocated prevention and intervention programs as the most cost-effective response to juvenile crime. Yet, despite the overwhelming evidence that reform is successful, resistance to it is rampant, and the brutal treatment of America's youth continues. The United States must find a way to reform the juvenile justice system once and for all.

Barry Krisberg, "Reforming Juvenile Justice," *The American Prospect*, August 14, 2005. Copyright copy; 2005 The American Prospect, Inc. All rights reserved. Reproduced with permission from *The American Prospect*, 11 Beacon Street, Suite 1120, Boston, MA 02108.

In 1899, Illinois and Colorado established a new "Children's Court." The idea was to substitute treatment and care for punishment of delinquent youths. These changes were promoted by child advocates such as the famous social activist Jane Addams [founder of Chicago's Hull House] and crusading judges like Denver's Ben Lindsey [who in 1900 established the juvenile court system], as well as influential women's organizations and bar associations. Over the next 20 years, the concept of a separate court system for minors spread to most states. Although the new children's court movement lacked adequate resources to fulfill its lofty mission, the intellectual promise was virtually unchallenged for two-thirds of the 20th century.

Several key assumptions lay behind the juvenile-court idea. First, children were not just "small adults," and they needed to be handled differently. Second, there was a need for specially trained legal and correctional professionals to work with minors. Third, placing children in adult prisons and jails made them more antisocial and criminal. And finally, the emerging science of rehabilitation could rescue many of these troubled young people from lives of crime. In the intervening years, a wealth of research has validated each of these premises.

The Demise of the Juvenile Justice System

Despite broad support within the academic, legal, and social-work professions, the ideal often failed to live up to its promise. Over time, the juvenile-justice system in many states reverted to the punitive approach it was designed to replace. Though they were often called "training schools," the institutions were juvenile prisons. And the premise that the court, by definition, was acting "in the best interest of the child" left young offenders without the rights guaranteed to adult criminal defendants. There were repeated accounts of abusive practices. The duration of confinement was often unrelated to the severity of the offense. Juvenile hearings were usually secret, with no written transcripts and no right to appeal. Minors were not provided legal counsel, there were no safeguards against self-incrimination, and offenders were denied liberty without the due process of law guaranteed by the U.S. Constitution.

A series of legal challenges culminated in the landmark 1967 Supreme Court decision *In Re Gault*. Writing for the Court, Justice Abe Fortas proclaimed, "Under our Constitution, the condition of being a boy does not justify a kangaroo court." Reviewing the case of 15-year-old Gerald Gault, who was sentenced to six years in an Arizona youth correctional facility for making an obscene phone call, the Court decreed that minors be afforded most of the due-process rights required in adult criminal courts.

Gault signaled a new era of reforms. One was a movement to divert as many youths as possible from the formal court system and to decriminalize "juvenile status offenses" such as truancy, running away, curfew violations, and incorrigibility. The 1970s witnessed widespread efforts to deinstitutionalize or "decarcerate" youngsters, moving them from secure detention centers and training schools to community-based programs that emphasized education and rehabilitation.

An Emphasis on Rehabilitation

The most dramatic example came in 1972 in Massachusetts, where a respected reformer closed all of the state juvenile facilities and started over. Jerome Miller had been recruited to the state Department of Youth Services (DYS) to clean up a range of scandals and abuses. He encountered an intransigent bureaucracy. Corrections officers opposed even such modest reforms as letting youngsters wear street clothing instead of prison uniforms, or not requiring that their heads be completely shaven. Undeterred, Miller decided to close down the state's network of jail-like training schools. As the young inmates of the notorious Lyman School were loaded onto a bus that would take them to dorms at the University of Massachusetts, to be housed temporarily until being reassigned to community programs, one top Miller deputy proclaimed to the shocked guards, "You can have the institutions; we are taking the kids."

The training schools were replaced with a diverse network of small residential programs, typically with 25 children or fewer, located closer to the youths' home communities. A range of nonresidential programs included day reporting centers and intensive home-based supervision. The DYS continued to operate about half of the most secure facilities. Private nonprofits were recruited to run the rest, as well as all of the community-based programs.

Although Miller left Massachusetts soon after becoming the department's youth-services commissioner, the Bay State continued to expand and refine the alternatives to the old prison-like training schools and never reopened the large juvenile institutions. Research by Harvard Law School and my organization, the National Council on Crime and Delinquency, showed that the Miller reforms successfully reduced the frequency and severity of new offenses of youth in the new programs compared with the training-school graduates.

As the Massachusetts model spread to many other states, Congress in 1974 created the federal Juvenile Justice and Delinquency Prevention Act, with bipartisan backing. The act established a federal Office of Juvenile Justice and Delinquency Prevention (OJJDP) to conduct research, provide training, and make grants to states and jurisdictions that voluntarily complied with the act's mandates. The new law required participating states to remove status offenders and dependency cases from secure confinement, and to separate juveniles from adults by "sight and sound" in correctional facilities. In 1980, the act was amended to require that participating states remove minors from jails. Forty-eight states participated.

Miller went on to implement variations of his Massachusetts reforms in Pennsylvania and Illinois. Other states that broadly followed Miller's model included jurisdictions as politically diverse as Utah, Missouri, and Vermont. Often, publicity about abusive conditions in state facilities and lawsuits in federal courts catalyzed these reforms. From 1980 into the 1990s, Colorado, Indiana, Oklahoma, Maryland, Louisiana, Florida, Georgia, Rhode Island, and New Jersey were among states that began closing large, prison-like youth facilities. For a time, it appeared that the Miller reforms would become the "gold standard" for juvenile corrections, as the federal OJJDP provided training and support to jurisdictions seeking to replicate the Massachusetts approach.

The Invention of the "Super-Predator"

The rejection in some quarters of a reform model reflects both ideological preconceptions and misinformation about juvenile crime. Rates of serious violent juvenile crime as measured by the National Crime Survey were relatively constant between 1973 and 1989, then briefly rose by more than one-third and peaked in 1993. Some cited demographics, as the children of the baby boomers reached their teenage years. Others pointed to an epidemic of crack cocaine that fueled urban violence, as well as high unemployment and declining economic prospects for low-skilled workers, especially among minority groups. No one really knows for sure. But fear of a violent juvenile crime wave led some to predict a new cohort of "super-predators." Conservative academics such as James Q. Wilson and John Dilulio and a small band of mainstream criminologists such as Alfred Blumstein and James Fox forecast societal disaster. Wilson predicted "30,000 more young muggers, killers, and thieves." Dilulio in 1990 foresaw another 270,000 violent juveniles by 2010. He warned of a "crime bomb" created by a generation of "fatherless, godless, and jobless [juvenile] super-predators."

The media hyped the story, and many elected officials exploited it. The citizenry was told about a generation of babies, born to "crack-addicted" mothers, who would possess permanent neurological damage, including the inability to feel empathy. The scientific evidence supporting this claim was nonexistent. More than 40 states made it easier to transfer children to adult criminal courts. Educators enacted "zero-tolerance" policies to make it easier to expel youngsters from school, and numerous communities adopted youth curfews. Many jurisdictions turned to metal detectors in public schools, random locker searches, drug tests for athletes, and mandatory school uniforms.

The panic was bipartisan. Every crime bill debated by Congress during the Clinton administration included new federal laws against juvenile crime. Paradoxically, as Attorney General Janet Reno advocated for wider and stronger social safety nets for vulnerable families. President Bill Clinton joined congressional leaders demanding tougher treatment of juvenile felons, including more incarceration in both the adult and youth correctional systems.

However, the much-advertised generation of superpredators never materialized. After 1993, rates of serious juvenile crime began a decade-long decline to historically low levels. And this juvenile-crime drop happened before the tougher juvenile penalties were even implemented. The fear-mongering social scientists had based their dire predictions on grossly inaccurate data and faulty reasoning, but the creators of the super-predator myth prevailed in the public-policy arena throughout most of the '90s. As we approached the centennial of the American juvenile court, it looked like the juvenile-justice ideal was dying.

The Ideal of Juvenile Justice Survives

Despite adverse political currents, the juvenile-justice ideal has received a new lease on life thanks to pioneering efforts by states and by foundations, as well as the continuing programmatic influence of the federal approach begun in the 1970s and expanded during the Clinton-Reno era.

One key initiative of the federal OJJDP is known as Balanced and Restorative Justice. This approach, now embraced by many jurisdictions, places a major value on involving victims in the rehabilitative process. By coming to terms with harm done to victims, the youthful offender is also offered a way to restore his or her role in the community.

Prevention was the most cost-effective response to youth crime.

The second significant federal program is the Justice Department's Comprehensive Strategy for Serious, Violent, and Chronic Juvenile Offenders, first adopted in 1993. The research showed that a very small number of offenders committed most serious juvenile crimes, and that identification and control of these "dangerous few" was key. However, unlike the response to the supposed super-predators, this strategy does not call for an across-the-board crackdown on at-risk youth. A comprehensive body of research assembled by two senior Justice Department juvenile-justice officials, John J. Wilson and James C. Howell, showed that prevention was the most cost-effective response to youth crime, and that strengthening the family and other core institutions was the most important goal for a youth-crime-control strategy.

The proposed comprehensive strategy was adopted by Reno as the official policy position of the Justice Department in all matters relating to juvenile crime, and the program was successfully implemented in more than 50 communities nationwide. The basic idea was to help local leaders build their youth-service systems to provide "the right service, for the right youth, at the right time." This collaborative planning process helped policy-makers and professionals to debunk the myths about juvenile crime and to learn about interventions that were proven, as well as to foster more cooperative activities among multiple agencies. Most important, the effort showed community participants how to effectively respond to juvenile lawbreaking without resorting to mass-incarceration policies.

A third major national reform movement was launched by the Annie E. Casey Foundation in 1992. The goal: to reduce the overuse of juvenile-detention facilities and to redirect funding toward more effective services for at-risk youngsters. The foundation also sought to improve the conditions of confinement for detained youth and to reduce the overrepresentation of minority youths in detention.

The Casey Foundation approach required a multiagency planning process and included the development of improved risk screening, expansion of options for most detained youths, and efforts to expedite the processing of cases. After initial demonstration projects, the foundation has expanded the program to scores of communities. It also offers technical assistance and convenes an annual meeting. At the last such convening, in San Francisco, more than 700 people from across the nation gathered to discuss ways to further reduce unnecessary juvenile detention. The original demonstration project has led to a vibrant national movement, which includes high-quality replication manuals and a documentary, plus academic and professional publications.

These approaches all require collaborations among many sectors of the community. They all employ data and evidence-based practices to guide the reform agenda. Diversity is recognized as vital because one-size-fits-all programs usually fail. Instead, they seek to create a comprehensive continuum of appropriate services. Preventive strategies and early interventions are viewed as far more cost-effective than punitive approaches. All these programs place a great emphasis on involving youth, plus their families and neighbors, in shaping solutions. The core values of the juvenile-justice ideal continue to live. Like the reform impulse of a century ago, the goal is to commit the juvenile-justice system to pursuing the best interests of the child, to strengthening family and community solutions to youth misconduct, and to emphasizing humane and fair treatment of the young.

Unlawful and brutal practices continue to plague youth correctional facilities in many states.

In spite of the promise embodied in approaches like these, unlawful and brutal practices continue to plague youth correctional facilities in many states. Some jurisdictions are being investigated by the federal government for statutory and constitutional violations of the rights of institutionalized minors. In other locales, advocates for young people are successfully litigating against youth detention and corrections facilities. At the same time, the political hysteria surrounding the superpredator myth appears to be in remission. The chorus is growing to reject approaches such as youth correctional boot camps or "scared straight" programs that use prison visits to try to frighten youngsters away from criminal lives. While some of these dangerous programs continue to exist, many jurisdictions have shut them down. There is growing awareness about the prevalence of mental illness among institutionalized youngsters and the emergence of several initiatives to better meet their health-care needs.

Small, community-based approaches that stress prevention, education, and restitution rather than prison-like punishment are simply better policy.

This year's [2005] most positive development was the Supreme Court's decision to end the death penalty for those younger than 18 at the time of their offense. But this progress does not minimize the severe problems of the juvenile-justice system. Funding for services for troubled young people in the juvenile-justice and child-welfare systems remains woefully inadequate. Young people still do not have anything resembling adequate legal representation. Too many continue to be banished to the criminal-court system and languish in adult prisons. And racism, sexism, and class biases continue to tarnish the promise of equal justice for all.

The Way Forward

This *American Prospect* special supplement includes reports from places as diverse as California, Texas, New Mexico, Missouri, and Louisiana. All suggest that reform coalitions, often with strange bedfellows, can acknowledge the superiority of the reform approach and change practices that dehumanize young people and fail to reduce juvenile crime. By now the evidence is clear: Small, community-based approaches that stress prevention, education, and restitution rather than prison-like punishment are simply better policy. At the same time, as Ellis Cose [author and columnist for *Newsweek*] recounts, racial disparities remain immense. And as Sam Rosenfeld [Web writer for *The American Prospect*] reports, far too many children who need mental-health services are being dumped into the juvenile-justice system.

The media continue to exaggerate the amount of violent crime committed by minors.

Given the overwhelming evidence that reform works, why is there continuing resistance? The answer to this question is complex. First and foremost, since the mid-'60s, crime policy in the United States has been heavily politicized. Democrats and Republicans have competed to position themselves as tough on crime. Being perceived as soft on juvenile offenders is considered a political liability. Second, the media continue to exaggerate the amount of violent crime committed by minors. Isolated stories about vicious crimes that are committed by very young adolescents are widely disseminated and become the grist for talk radio and other media commentary. The simplistic solution has been that tough responses to juvenile crime will deter youthful offenders.

Resistance to proven juvenile-justice models often comes from public-employee unions that fear the loss of jobs as traditional youth correctional facilities are downsized and some funding goes to community-based organizations. Also, severe state and local budget problems have led to a retrenchment in needed services, even as more innovative juvenile-justice models could actually save money. In some locales, organizations purporting to represent families of crime victims have lobbied for tougher penalties for juvenile offenders.

Progressive reforms are often undercut by entrenched biases about the predominantly poor and minority families caught up in the juvenile-justice system. These racial, ethnic, and class prejudices are too often reinforced by media reports that breed fear among the electorate about the "barbarians at the gates." As long as economic and fiscal pressures fuel anxiety over immigrants, the increased competition for jobs, and the deteriorating public-school system, it will be hard to generate compassionate and rational responses for youthful lawbreakers.

Jerome Miller once observed that the history of juvenile justice reflects a pattern of abuse and scandal followed by humanistic changes, but then a return to the previous conditions and bad practices. In a new millennium, one can only hope that proponents of the juvenile-justice ideal can figure out how to end this tragic cycle.

Organizations to Contact

The editors have compiled the following list of organizations concerned with the issues debated in this book. The descriptions are derived from materials provided by the organizations. All have publications or information available for interested readers. The list was compiled on the date of publication of the present volume; the information provided here may change. Be aware that many organizations take several weeks or longer to respond to inquiries, so allow as much time as possible.

Campaign for Youth Justice
1012 14th St. NW, Suite 610, Washington, DC   20005
(202) 558-3580 • (202) 386-9807
e-mail: info@campaign4youthjustice.org
Web site: www.campaignforyouthjustice.org

The Campaign for Youth Justice is committed to providing the most recent, reliable, and relevant research on the practice of trying, sentencing, and incarcerating youth under the age of eighteen in the adult criminal justice system. Among the publications that can be found on its Web site are the reports "Childhood on Trial: The Failure of Trying and Sentencing Youth in Adult Criminal Court," and "A Capital Offense: Youth in DC's Adult Criminal Justice System and Strategies for Reform."

Center for the Study and Prevention of Violence (CSPV)
Institute of Behavioral Science, Boulder, CO   80309-0438
(303) 492-8465 • fax: (303) 443-3297
Web site: www.colorado.edu/cspv

The CSPV was founded in 1992 to provide information and assistance to organizations that are dedicated to preventing violence—particularly youth violence. Its publications include the papers "Drugs, Alcohol, and Adolescent Violence" and "Youth Participation in Hate-Motivated Crimes."

Center on Juvenile and Criminal Justice (CJCJ)
54 Dore St., San Francisco, CA   94103
(415) 621-5661 • fax: (415) 621-5466
Web site: www.cjcj.org

The CJCJ is a private, nonprofit organization advocating reduced reliance on incarceration as a solution to social problems. The center provides direct services, technical assistance,
and policy research in the criminal justice field. Publications
available online include "California Youth Crime Declines:
The Untold Story," "From Houses of Refuge to 'Youth
Corrections': Same Story, Different Day," and "Why Are We So
Punitive? Some Observations on Recent Incarceration Trends."

Council of Juvenile Correctional Administrators (CJCA)
170 Forbes Rd., Suite 106, Braintree, MA   02184
(781) 843-2663
Web site: www.cjca.net

The Council of Juvenile Correctional Administrators is dedicated to improving youth correctional services and practices
through the exchange of ideas among correction system administrators. It seeks to educate the public about juvenile justice and corrections, with emphasis on treatment and rehabilitation. CJCA provides information through its annual
publication *CJCA Yearbook (Juvenile Corrections: A National
Perspective)* and quarterly newsletters.

Criminal Justice Legal Foundation (CJLF)
PO Box 1199, Sacramento, CA   95812
(916) 446-0345
e-mail: cjlf@cljf.org/mail2CJLF.htm
Web site: www.cjlf.org

The CJLF is a nonprofit, public interest organization dedicated to balancing the rights of crime victims and the crimi-
nally accused. The foundation's purpose is to assure that
people who are guilty of committing crimes receive swift and
certain punishment in an orderly and thoroughly constitu-

tional manner. To that end its attorneys introduce scholarly friend-of-the-court briefs in criminal cases before state and federal courts of appeals. Publications include the quarterly newsletter, *Advisory*, and various articles concerning the criminal justice system.

Joint Center for Poverty Research (JCPR)
Northwestern University, Institute for Policy Research
Evanston, IL   60208
(847) 491-3395 • fax: (847) 491-9916
Web site: www.jcpr.org

The JCPR is a national, interdisciplinary academic research center that seeks to advance understanding of the effects of poverty in America, including high rates of juvenile crime. Through social science research, the center attempts to influence the discussion and formation of policy, and the behavior and beliefs of individuals and organizations. Publications available include a bimonthly newsletter, working papers, policy briefs, and online books and reports.

Justice Policy Institute (JPI)
1003 K St. NW, Suite 500, Washington, DC   20001
(202) 558-7974 • fax: (202) 558-7978
Web site: www.justicepolicy.org

The Justice Policy Institute is a think tank committed to reducing society's reliance on incarceration. It generates pragmatic approaches to problems within both juvenile and criminal justice systems. A collection of publications located on its Web site include fact sheets and the report "The Consequences Aren't Minor: The Impact of Trying Youth as Adults and Strategies for Reform."

Juvenile Law Center (JLC)
The Philadelphia Building, Philadelphia, PA   19107
(215) 625-0551; (800) 875-8887 • fax: (215) 625-2808
Web site: www.jlc.org

The Juvenile Law Center works to ensure that youths in the juvenile justice system are treated fairly, in particular that they have access to competent counsel. JLC emphasizes youths' access to education and health care, and also focuses attention on disproportionate minority contact with the justice system. The center distributes a wide range of publications, testifies at public forums, advises the executive and legislative branches of state and federal governments on the effects of proposed legislation or regulations on children, serves as a resource to the media, and answers inquiries from the general public. Its Web site offers links to a broad range of articles and reports on juvenile justice issues.

National Center for Juvenile Justice (NCJJ)
3700 South Water St., Suite 200, Pittsburgh, PA   15203
(412) 227-6950 • fax: (412) 227-6955
Web site: www.ncjj.org

The National Center for Juvenile Justice is a private, nonprofit research organization dedicated to the improvement of the juvenile and family court system. Founded in 1973, the center compiles statistics and conducts and sponsors independent and original research on topics related directly and indirectly to the field of juvenile justice. Publications available include *Juvenile Offenders and Victims: 2006 National Report; Advancing Accountability: Moving Toward Victim Restoration*; and the monthly "NCJJ Snapshot," which summarizes current legal issues relating to how children and families are handled in juvenile and family courts.

National Center on Institutions and Alternatives (NCIA)
7222 Ambassador Rd., Baltimore, MD   21244
(410) 265-1490
Web site: www.ncia.org

The NCIA promotes innovative concepts in criminal and juvenile justice, providing professional research, mining, and technical assistance in support of alternative, community-based programs for nonviolent criminal offenders. The center's services focus on four major areas: criminal justice, mental health, education, and advocacy. Links can be found on its Web site to articles, including "When Hard Time Becomes Just a Waste" and "Juvenile Justice: Facts vs. Anger."

National Council of Juvenile and Family Court Judges (NCJFCJ)

PO Box 8970, Reno, NV 89507
(775) 784-6012 • fax: (775) 784-6628
e-mail: staff@ncjfcj.org
Web site: www.ncjfcj.org

Founded in 1937 by a group of judges dedicated to improving the effectiveness of the nation's juvenile court, NCJFCJ provides training, technical assistance, and research to judges, social and mental health workers, police, and others involved in the juvenile justice system. Among its publications are *Children's Exposure to Domestic Violence: A Guide to Research and Resources; Juvenile and Family Court Journal: Child Trauma*; and *Juvenile Delinquency Guidelines: Improving Court Practice in Juvenile Delinquency Cases.*

National Council on Crime and Delinquency (NCCD)

1970 Broadway, Suite 500, Oakland, CA 94612
(510) 208-0500 • fax: (510) 208-0511
Web site: www.nccd-crc.org

The NCCD assists government, law enforcement, and community organizations in developing programs to address juvenile justice problems. It conducts research, promotes reform initiatives, and works to prevent and reduce juvenile crime and delinquency. The council is launching an initiative to increase health and mental health services for youth in the juvenile justice system, specifically those in detention, local correctional programs, or in reentry status. Among its publications is the bulletin "Preventing Delinquency Through Improved Child Protection Services."

National Crime Prevention Council (NCPC)
2345 Crystal Dr., 5th Floor, Arlington, VA   22202
(202) 466-6272 • Fax: (202) 296-1356
Web site: www.ncpc.org

The council works to prevent juvenile crime and to build safer neighborhoods. Its Youth as Resources program, which encourages local youngsters to implement projects to help their communities, is based on the premise that young people have the desire and capability to address many youth crime problems on their own. The council's publications include the monthly *Catalyst Newsletter* and the report "Making Children, Families, and Communities Safer from Violence."

National Juvenile Defender Center (NJDC)
1350 Connecticut Ave. NW, Suite 304
Washington, DC   20086
(202) 452-0010 • fax: (202) 452-1205
e-mail: inquiries@njdc.info
Web site: www.njdc.info

In 2005 the National Juvenile Defender Center separated from the American Bar Association to become an independent organization. NJDC provides support to public defenders, appointed counsel, law school clinical programs, and nonprofit law centers to ensure quality representation in urban, suburban, rural, and tribal areas. NJDC offers a wide range of integrated services to juvenile defenders, including training, technical assistance, advocacy, networking, collaboration, capacity building, and coordination. The center produces reports, training guides, and fact sheets, including the "2007 Juvenile Defender Resource Guide," and "Principles in Practice."

Office of Juvenile Justice and Delinquency Prevention (OJJDP)
810 Seventh St. NW, Washington, DC   20531
(202) 307-5911
Web site: www.ojjdp.ncjrs.org

The OJJDP was established by the Juvenile Justice and Delinquency Prevention Act of 2002. Its missions are to support state and local programs that prevent delinquent behavior, to promote public safety by encouraging accountability for acts of juvenile delinquency, and to assist state and local governments in addressing juvenile crime through technical assistance, research, training, evaluation, and the dissemination of information. Among other publications, the agency publishes the newsletter *OJJDP News @ a Glance*, fact sheets, bulletins, and the teleconference "Addressing the Needs of Juvenile Status Offenders and their Families."

Youth Law Center (YLC)
200 Pine St., Suite 300, San Francisco, CA   94104
(415) 543-3379 • fax: (415) 956-9022
e-mail: info@ylc.org
Web site: www.ylc.org

The Youth Law Center works to protect children in the juvenile justice system from abuse and neglect and to ensure that they are provided with the conditions and services they need to grow into healthy, productive adults. Its publications, catalogued on its Web site, address the topics of juvenile justice and youth rights, including *And Justice for Some: Differential Treatment of minority Youth in the Juvenile Justice System* and *A Call for Justice: An Assessment of Access to Counsel and Quality of Representation in Delinquency Proceedings*.

Bibliography

Books

Gordon Bazemore and Mara Schiff — *Juvenile Justice Reform and Retorative Justice: Building Theory and Policy from Practice.* Portland, OR: Willan, 2005.

A. Blumstein and J. Wallman — *The Crime Drop in America.* New York: Cambridge University Press, 2006.

Joan Jacobs Brumberg — *Kansas Charley: The Boy Murderer.* New York: Penguin Books, 2004.

Meda Chesney-Lind and Randall G. Shelden — *Girls, Delinquency, and Juvenile Justice.* Stamford, CT: Wadsworth, 2003.

R.R. Corrado, R. Roesch, S.D. Hart, J.K. Gierowski, eds. — *Multi-Problem Violent Youth: A Foundation for Comparative Research on Needs, Interventions and Outcomes.* Amsterdam: IOS, 2002.

Michael Corriero — *Judging Children as Children: A Proposal for a Juvenile Justice System.* Philadelphia: Temple University Press, 2006.

Thomas Grisso and Robert Schwartz, eds. — *Youth on Trial: A Developmental Perspective on Juvenile Justice.* Chicago: University of Chicago Press, 2003.

Thomas Grisso, Gina Vincent, and Daniel Seagrave, eds. *Mental Health Screening and Assessment in Juvenile Justice.* New York: Guilford, 2005.

Darnell F. Hawkins and Kimberly Kempf-Leonard, eds. *Our Children, Their Children: Confronting Racial and Ethnic Differences in American Juvenile Justice.* Chicago: University of Chicago Press, 2005.

K. Heilbrun, N.E. Goldstein, and R.E. Redding *Juvenile Delinquency: Assessment, Prevention, and Intervention.* New York: Oxford University Press, 2005.

Margaret Jasper *Your Child's Legal Rights: An Overview.* New York: Oxford University Press, 2003.

Barry Krisberg *Juvenile Justice: Redeeming Our Children.* Thousand Oaks, CA: Sage, 2004.

Aaron Kupchik *Judging Juveniles: Prosecuting Adolescents in Adult and Juvenile Courts.* New York: New York University Press, 2006.

Clarence Augustus Martin *Juvenile Justice: Process and Systems.* Thousand Oaks, CA: Sage, 2005.

David L. Meyers *Boys Among Men: Trying and Sentencing Juveniles as Adults.* Westport, CT: Praeger, 2005.

Allison Morris and Gabrielle Maxwell, eds. *Restorative Justice for Juveniles: Conferencing, Mediation and Circles.* Portland, OR: Hart, 2003.

Joycelyn M. Pollock — *Ethical Dilemmas and Decisions in Criminal Justice.* Stamford, CT: Wadsworth, 2006.

Declan Roche — *Accountability in Restorative Justice.* New York: Oxford University Press, 2003.

Laurie Schaffner — *Girls in Trouble with the Law.* Piscataway, NJ: Rutgers University Press, 2006.

Larry J. Siegel, Brandon C. Welsh, and Joseph J. Senna — *Juvenile Delinquency: Theory, Practice, and Law.* Stamford, CT: Wadsworth, 2005.

Robert W. Taylor, Eric J. Fritsch, and Tory J. Caeti — *Juvenile Justice: Policies, Programs, and Practices.* Columbus, OH: McGraw-Hill, 2006.

Franklin E. Zimring — *American Juvenile Justice.* New York: Oxford University Press, 2005.

Franklin E. Zimring — *An American Travesty: Legal Responses to Adolescent Sexual Offending.* Chicago: University of Chicago Press, 2004.

Periodicals

Amnesty International and Human Rights Watch — "The Rest of Their Lives: Life Without Parole for Child Offenders in the United States," www.hrw.org, October 2005.

Mary Beckman   "Crime, Culpability and the Adolescent Brain," *Science Magazine*, July 30, 2004.

Robert Blecker   "A Poster Child for Us," *Judicature*, March–April 2006.

Robert H. Bork   "Travesty Time, Again: In Its Death-Penalty Decision, the Supreme Court Hits a New Low," *National Review*, March 28, 2005.

Bruce Bower   "Teen Brains on Trial: The Science of Neural Development Tangles with the Juvenile Death Penalty," *Science News Online*, May 8, 2004.

Craig M. Bradley   "The Right Decision on the Juvenile Death Penalty," *Judicature*, March–April 2006.

Michelle Calderon   "Age as Criminal Defense," AnaiRhoads.org, October 27, 2005.

Campaign for Youth Justice   "New Report: Legal Loophole Leads to Explosion of Youth in Adult Jails; Abuse and Isolation Rampant; Majority Held for Nonviolent Crimes," *Justice Policy Institute*, March 21, 2007.

Tom Carter   "Thousands of Young Offenders in US Face Life Behind Bars," World Socialist Web Site (wsws.org), October 15, 2005.

Richard C. Dieter   "Court Must End Death Penalty for Children," *Los Angeles Daily Journal*, February 19, 2004.

Marilyn Elias   "Is Adult Prison Best for Juveniles?" *USA Today*, September 20, 2006.

Julian D. Ford, John F. Chapman, Josephine Hawke, and David Albert   "Trauma Among Youth in the Juvenile Justice System: Critical Issues and New Directions," National Center for Mental Health and Juvenile Justice Research and Program Brief, June 2007.

Andy Furillo   "Accord Reached on Young Prisoners," *San Diego Union-Tribune*, July 6, 2007.

M. Gardner and L. Steinberg   "Peer Influence on Risk-Taking, Risk Preference, and Risky Decision-Making in Adolescence and Adulthood: An Experimental Study," *Developmental Psychology*, 2005.

Anemona Hartocollis   "4 Harlem Boys Will Be Tried as Juveniles," *New York Times*, April 15, 2006.

Andy Humbles   "Prosecutors Weigh Merits of Charging Kids as Adults," *(Nashville) Tennessean*, February 2, 2004.

Mary Ellen Johnson   "Life Without Parole Is Retribution," *The New Abolitionist*, May 2007.

Rachel King   "Killing Kids," www.TomPaine.com, November 18, 2004.

MacArthur Foundation Research Network on Adolescent Development and Juvenile Justice "Issue Brief 5: The Changing Borders of Juvenile Justice: Transfer of Adolescents to the Adult Criminal Court," www.adjj.org, 2006.

MacArthur Foundation Research Network on Adolescent Development and Juvenile Justice "Issue Brief 3: Less Guilty by Reason of Adolescence," www.adjj.org, 2006.

Dennis Maloney "Restorative Community Service: Earning Redemption, Gaining Skills, and Proving Worth," *Reclaiming Children and Youth*, Winter 2007.

Terry A. Maroney "Should Juveniles Be Tried as Adults?" *(Nashville) Tennessean*, January 7, 2007.

Daniel A. Munz "Troubled Teens Need a Better Judicial System," *Yale Herald*, January 30, 2004.

National Center for Youth Law "Yee Bill Would Reform Life Sentences for Minors," www.youthlaw .org, 2007.

Nancy Rodriguez "Restorative Justice at Work: Examining the Impact of Restorative Justice Resolution on Juvenile Recidivism," *Crime & Delinquency*, July 2007.

Sam Rosenfeld   "The Era of Get-Tough Juvenile Justice Is Also the Era of Managed Care, and Children with Mental-Health Needs Are Caught in the Crossfire," *The American Prospect*, August 15, 2005.

Noaki Schwartz   "Child Advocates Call for Flexible Juvenile Justice System," *(South Florida) Sun-Sentinel*, February 8, 2004.

USA Today   "Many Teens Tried as Adults with Little Understanding of Process," March 3, 2003.

Index